Margaret Fuller: An Uncommon Woman

by

Adele Fasick

MONGANBOOKS 2012

Table of Contents

Prologue

In a gloomy gray palazzo overlooking a narrow street in Rome, an American woman bent over a table writing a long letter to the *New York Tribune*. "May 6, 1849, I write to you from a barricaded Rome..."

Rome was under siege. Outside the streets were strangely deserted. A hush had fallen as Romans wondered what the French troops massed outside the city walls would do next. Suddenly the boom of cannon broke the silence. Italy, like most of Europe, was in turmoil that year. A new democratic government had been installed in Rome, but many aristocrats did not accept the idea of ordinary people taking power. Most American and British travelers, afraid of being caught in a war, had left the city. But the woman writing the letter, Margaret Fuller, was determined to see the revolution first hand.

She had spent several nights in a hospital treating the wounded Italian fighters and was exhausted from the strain. Although the light grew dim and her hand became tired holding the pen, Margaret kept writing, "War near at hand," she wrote, was "even more dreadful than I had fancied it....I have for the first time, seen what wounded men suffer." Her friends might flee from the city, but Margaret wanted Americans to know what was happening.

Margaret was the first American woman to write news reports regularly from a foreign country. Most Americans could not believe a woman would leave home to live in Europe and earn money by writing for a newspaper. The proper role for a woman was to get married and devote her life to her husband and children. But Margaret was different. She was determined to make her mark in the world, and she succeeded. She became one of the most influential literary figures in New England. Then she moved to New York to write for the *New York Tribune*. Later she traveled to Europe as a reporter and became a friend of men who were plotting revolutions in several countries. What was it about Margaret that made her do things other women never tried and most men frowned upon?

Chapter 1: Massachusetts Beginnings

Massachusetts in 1810 was a green and largely rural state. Boston had a population just over 30,000, many of them descendents of the Puritans who had settled the area 200 years earlier. Harvard University in Cambridge, eight miles from the city and across the Charles River, was already a center of New England intellectual life. Only a generation separated the citizens of Massachusetts from the revolution that had given them freedom from Britain. Many people could remember the exciting events of 1775, just 35 years earlier, when Patrick Henry declared "Give me liberty or give me death…" and Paul Revere took his famous ride. America had become a country by means of a Constitution written in 1787 and a Bill of Rights adopted in 1791. No one was quite sure whether the new country would survive, and many people were still trying to get used to the idea of living in a Republic.

The new country needed educated men of character to determine its future, and young Timothy Fuller was prepared to do just that. As the son of a clergyman in Princeton, Massachusetts, he had grown up with the ambition of attending Harvard, becoming a lawyer, and serving his country. By the time he was thirty, he had graduated from Harvard, opened a law practice, and become an active participant in Massachusetts politics. He had also met his future wife, Margarett [sic] Crane of Canton, Massachusetts, and in 1809 he married his young bride, who had just turned twenty. Her background was similar to his and she was an attractive and charming young woman who stood five feet ten inches tall, a head taller than her slight, wiry husband. Their marriage was to prove a congenial and satisfying one for both of them. They started married life in a house in Cambridgeport (now part of Cambridge) close to the harbor which handled most of the goods destined for Boston.

On May 23, 1810, the couple's first child was born, a daughter whom they named Sarah Margaret Fuller. Although most men of the time looked forward to their firstborn son, Timothy was deeply satisfied with just being a father. He planted two elm trees in front of the house to commemorate the event and determined to play an active role in her upbringing. For a while it seemed Sarah Margaret might be an only child, as a younger sister died before she was two, and it wasn't until 1815 that the Fuller's first surviving son, Eugene, was born and two years later another son, William. Margaret was well into her teens before the family was complete with the birth of two more boys and a sister, Ellen.

Before Margaret was four years old, her father started teaching her to read. She was a bright child who learned easily. Within a few months she was reading stories and enjoying them. Almost as soon as she had mastered reading in English, Timothy decided to teach her Latin. By the time she was six years old, Margaret was spending her days bent over a book instead of playing with other children. Her mother was busy with a new baby boy and no one noticed that Sarah Margaret was often lonely and unhappy. *Amo, amas, amat* she would repeat to herself as she struggled to remember the complicated grammar of Latin. Timothy, delighted that she learned so easily, encouraged her to begin reading Latin texts about the heroes and warriors of ancient Rome. He was unaware that at night Margaret sometimes had nightmares about the wars she read about in her Latin history books.

In 1817, when Margaret was seven years old, Timothy Fuller was elected to Congress and traveled to Washington D.C. to take up his duties. He was determined to continue teaching Margaret even though he was away much of the time. He told her which books she should read and insisted she write regular letters to him about her reading. Young Margaret was a faithful correspondent and tried hard to please her father. In March 1818 she wrote: *I was very much disappointed not to receive a letter from you....I think I have improved a good deal in writing and I can sing one part while Aunt Abigail sings another. I guess you will buy my pianneforte.* A few months later she reported *"Now I will tell you what I study. Latin twice a week and Arithmetick when Aunt Elizabeth is here."* (Fuller and Hudspeth 1983, 1:84)

Margaret had lessons with her two aunts and her mother. In the fall of 1819, she began to attend the newly formed Cambridge Port Grammar School run by a young Harvard graduate named John Dickinson. Timothy continued to recommend books to his young daughter and insisted that she write reports for him of her reading. In December 1819, she wrote to him:

I enclose you my composition and specimen of writing. I assure you I wrote the former off much better and made almost as many corrections as your critical self would were you at home. But Mr. kept the theme I corrected as he always does the theme which is written at the end of the quarter. I think this is one of the best themes I ever wrote. (Fuller and Hudspeth 1983, 1:91)

Eventually Timothy relinquished his role as chief tutor to his daughter and Margaret started attending school regularly. She and the other girls at the Cambridge Port Private Grammar School were part time students, while the boys went all day because they were preparing to enter Harvard College. The girls were allowed to learn Latin with the boys, but were sent home when it was time for mathematics and Greek. Margaret excelled at the lessons, but she soon realized that making friends was harder for her than doing class work. She longed to impress the other students and make them like her, but she had no idea how to go about it, so she was often lonely.

Margaret got along well with many adult friends of her family who admired her precocious abilities, although some people thought her too forward. She was well aware of how well read she was and did not hesitate to correct even adults when they misquoted a book or misstated a fact. Also around this time, she decided that the name her parents had given her — Sarah Margaret — was not suitable. She though Sarah was "a proper good old maidish name" and preferred to have her friends call her Margaret. She remained Margaret for the rest of her life except to her father who did not like having his mother's name dropped.

Disturbed by Margaret's lack of social graces, her parents decided to send her to a boarding school to be with girls of her own age and learn more about manners and deportment. They sent her to Miss Susan Prescott's Young Ladies' Seminary at Groton, a small country town about forty miles from Cambridge. Perhaps

Timothy regretted having encouraged Margaret to be so outstandingly brilliant. At any rate, he and his wife agreed on a conventional girls' boarding school where they expected Margaret would learn a smattering of subjects useful for a girl, and would be taught to behave in a quiet, ladylike way.

When Margaret arrived at Miss Prescott's school, she found that none of the other girls knew nearly as much about history and languages as she did, but they knew far more about fashionable clothes and society. Once again she felt lonely and out of place. Determined to make friends, Margaret tried to dazzle the other girls with her knowledge. Years later, she wrote a story, "Mariana", based on her life at the boarding school. There is no way to know how close this story is to what actually happened, but it offers the only clues we have to how Margaret interacted with her fellow students. In later years, Margaret told people the story of Mariana was autobiographical. It was probably an exaggeration of what happened at the school, but it gives a clear picture of how Margaret remembered her school experiences.

In the story, Mariana is a vivid and dramatic girl who tells exciting stories, makes up fanciful dances, and persuades some of the others to put on plays. These plays become more important than anything else in her life. She loves wearing costumes and make-up, although respectable girls in those days never used cosmetics. The other students were content to follow Mariana's lead for weeks and months, but finally they grew tired of her exaggerated moods. Mariana began to wear rouge on her cheeks every day as if she were an actress. The girls, and even the teachers laughed and joked about this, but

Mariana paid no attention. At last, the others decided to teach her a lesson. One day when she went into the dining room, she looked around the table and saw that every girl had a bright spot of rouge on her cheeks. No one said anything, but Mariana knew the girls were laughing at her. She refused to laugh with them but ate her dinner silently. Afterwards she went to her room and fell into such a fit of grief and anger that she became ill and was sick for days. When she recovered, she gave up the theatricals and the rouge and became quiet and studious.

Margaret wasn't always unhappy at school. Some of the students were friendly and one of her favorite teachers, Miss Prescott, recognized Margaret's gifts and became a lifelong friend. But there's no question it was hard to be the smartest girl in the school. Margaret enjoyed being recognized as a brilliant scholar, but as she turned fifteen, she must have wondered whether she would ever be able to combine brilliance with popularity.

Chapter 2: Apprenticeship (1826-1835)

After Margaret finished one year at boarding school, her formal education ended. She was fifteen, an age at which many boys went to Harvard College but there was no college for Margaret. She was needed at home because her mother was pregnant again and missed her eldest daughter's company and her help with the younger children. Timothy agreed that domestic duties were more important than school. Margaret did not object to leaving Miss Prescott's school and probably believed she would learn more at home than by going to classes there. When she moved back home, she attended Greek classes at Cambridgeport Grammar school, studied on her own, helped her mother, and began teaching her younger brothers and sister. Life was busy but sometimes dull. In one letter Margaret wrote, *"I have escaped from the parlor where I've been sitting the livelong evening playing auditor to Judge Weston, his jokes and anecdotes are pleasant enough but I fairly ache sitting three hours in boarding-school attitude hemming a ruffle and saying never a word."* (Fuller and Hudspeth 1983, 1:163-4)

Margaret enjoyed learning, and she was ambitious. *"I am determined on distinction,"* she wrote to Miss Prescott. (Fuller and Hudspeth 1983, 1:152) She set herself an ambitious program of studying the classics and reported her progress to Miss Prescott. Her letters were filled with happy accounts of her reading, *"I have not had my mind so exercised in months,"* (Fuller and Hudspeth 1983, 1:155) she wrote, but she longed to have people to share her interests; *"[I] feel an aching wish for* some person with whom I might talk fully and openly." Miss Prescott remained a good friend and correspondent although after she married in 1829, her letters became less frequent.

Meanwhile Margaret's life was changing. Timothy Fuller left Congress and set up a law practice in Cambridge. With a new baby in the house, he decided the family needed more room so they left the Cambridgeport house and moved to Cambridge, which was home to many families connected with Harvard.

Margaret was eager to find friends her own age, but her rigorous program of self-education kept her busy. As she reported to Miss Prescott:

You keep me to my promise of giving you some sketch of my pursuits. I rise a little before five, walk an hour, and then practise on the piano, till seven, when we breakfast. Next I read French,--Sismondi's Literature of the South of Europe,-- till eight, then two or three lectures in Brown's Philosophy. About half-past nine I go to Mr. Perkins's school and study Greek till twelve, when, the school being dismissed, I recite, go home, and practise again till dinner, at two. Sometimes, if the conversation is very agreeable, I lounge for half an hour over the dessert, though rarely so lavish of time. Then, when I can, I read two hours in Italian, but I am often interrupted. At six, I walk, or take a drive. Before going to bed, I play or sing, for half an hour or so, to make all sleepy, and, about eleven, retire to write a little while in my journal, exercises on what I have read, or a series of characteristics which I am filling up according to advice. Thus, you see, I am learning Greek, and making acquaintance with metaphysics, and French and Italian literature. (Fuller, Channing, and Emerson 1857)

To a modern eye, this schedule looks daunting and it is small wonder that many of her peers in

Cambridge found her learning rather threatening. Her appearance did not help in her search for friends; she was a large girl with a matronly figure and a rather florid complexion. Because she was very nearsighted, she tended to peer at people when she spoke to them. Her mother and her younger sister were both considered beauties, and Margaret could not compare with them as her father frequently reminded her. Like most teenage girls, she found it difficult to forget her appearance and she struggled to make her intellectual qualities compensate for her looks.

Margaret may not have been beautiful, but she had a flair for the dramatic and she attracted attention. Friends remembered that during these years she often wore a hooded cloak when she went to the circulating library in one of the small shops in town. She would take off her cloak, fill the hood with books, swing it over her shoulder and carry her books home. One friend said, "We all wished that our mothers would let us have hooded cloaks, that we might carry our books that way." (Higginson 1899, 25). Margaret inspired awe in many teenagers and some circulated a rumor that she could rock the cradle, read a book, eat an apple, and knit a stocking all at the same time.

The boys Margaret went to school with in Cambridge included Oliver Wendell Holmes and his younger brother John. Oliver Holmes, father of the famous Justice Oliver Wendell Holmes, Jr., was himself a well-known author in later years. He remembered Margaret well and sixty years later wrote of an incident when some of the school essays were sent to his father for review. Oliver took the opportunity to read Margaret's paper and found the first sentence was "It is a trite remark." He stopped reading, "Alas, I did not know what trite meant" a "crushing discovery" that he never forgot. (Capper 1992, 46)

Richard Henry Dana, author of the classic *Two Years Before the Mast*, who became a prominent lawyer supporting the rights of seamen and the abolition of slavery, was another student at the school. James Freeman Clarke, later an important religious leader and writer, and a lifelong friend of Margaret was also in the group. When their schooling was finished, the boys all went to Harvard College to train for professions, while the girls stayed at home to study on their own and prepare to be wives and mothers.

James Freeman Clarke, a distant relative, remained close to Margaret and they exchanged many confidential letters, which Margaret sometimes signed, "Your cousin only thirty-seven degrees removed." Clarke became fascinated by Margaret's ideas and the two met or exchanged letters almost every day. Clarke later wrote of Margaret:

Margaret possessed, in a greater degree than any person I ever knew, the power of so magnetizing others, when she wished, by the power of her mind, that they would lay open to her all the secrets of their nature. She had an infinite curiosity to know individuals,--not the vulgar curiosity which seeks to find out the circumstances of their outward lives, but that which longs to understand the inward springs of thought and action in their souls. (Fuller, Channing, and Emerson 1857)

Margaret revealed many of her hopes and disillusions, questioning Clarke about himself, and when he answered, interpreting his responses and questioning some more. (Bolster 1954, 58) Both James

Clarke and Margaret expected a great deal of intimacy from their friends and Clarke even asked Margaret to comment on his recent love affair with a mutual friend. Margaret declined the opportunity and wrote: *I cannot promise you any limitless confidence, but I can promise that no timid caution, no haughty dread shall prevent my telling you the truth of my thoughts on any subject we may have in common. Will this satisfy you? Oh let it! Suffer me to know you.* (Fuller and Hudspeth 1983, 1:163)

Clarke also introduced Margaret to German literature and encouraged her to learn German, a language not generally studied at that time when French and Italian were considered culturally more important. The study of German was growing, however, ever since Charles Follen was appointed the first Professor of German at Harvard in 1825. (He was also noted for introducing the Christmas tree to New England.) The study of German was controversial in Unitarian circles with conservatives charging that German thinkers were introducing licentiousness in literature, skepticism in theology and a dangerous mystical subjectivism in philosophy. (Capper 1992, 115) How could Margaret resist finding out for herself? She learned German quickly and according to Clarke within three months was reading German classics. Margaret became especially intrigued with the writings of Johann Wolfgang von Goethe and Clarke encouraged her to try translating some of them.

Several of Margaret's friends during these years were older women who had more time to pay attention to a teenager than her own busy mother had. Most notable among these was Eliza Farrar, an English Quaker who had moved to Boston to live with relatives when her father lost his fortune. There she married the widowed John Farrar, a popular professor of mathematics at Harvard. The couple had no children and Eliza enjoyed meeting her husband's students and their friends. She recognized Margaret's intellectual promise, but also saw her social ineptitude. She set herself the task of making Margaret "less abrupt, less self-asserting….She had [Margaret] constantly at her own house, reformed her hairdresser…took her to make calls and took her on journeys." (Higginson 1899, 36)

As she entered her twenties, Margaret's social life grew more active. Cambridge was a small community and she met many of its most famous citizens including Elizabeth Palmer Peabody, who ran an influential bookstore and had plans to start a magazine, as well as Lydia Maria Child, already a novelist and beginning to be active in the anti-slavery cause.

By 1833, Timothy Fuller was becoming tired of public life. Perhaps his failed campaign to become Lieutenant Governor of Massachusetts had something to do with that. He decided to buy a farm in the country and devote himself to writing a history of the United States. The farm he chose was near Groton where Margaret had spent a year at school. The school itself had been closed when Miss Prescott married and moved out of the area. This made the town seem more isolated than ever. In those days thirty-five miles was a long way to travel, so Margaret would have few chances to visit her friends or go to the bookstores she loved in Boston.

The two brothers closest to Margaret in age did not like the idea of living on a farm and both of them left the family to seek work in Boston and New Orleans when they graduated from Harvard. Margaret would have liked an independent life too, but it was impossible for a young woman to move away from her family. Instead, she became the official head of a family school and began systematically educating the three younger boys and her sister, Ellen. During the second year in Groton, several neighboring children came to the Fuller home for Margaret's school and she found she had full time employment.

Margaret's father paid her for teaching just as he would have paid any other teacher. At last, she was able to start saving money for a trip to Italy, which she had dreamed about for years. Young women in those days did not go to Europe alone, so Margaret knew she would have to find people to travel with her. An opportunity came when John and Eliza Farrar suggested she go to Europe with them for a yearlong tour of the continent. A trip with the Farrars would be the ideal way for Margaret to travel and she worked hard to save money.

Margaret made the most of her time in Groton. Although she claimed her teaching took up most of the day and that she could not get books to read, the list of her reading was remarkably long. She spent much of her time studying German, reading and annotating the Goethe books she was able to obtain. She wrote many letters to her Cambridge friends discussing possibilities for future writing and teaching. When James Freeman Clarke moved to Kentucky to take up a ministry in Lexington, she suggested to him that she might be able to go west as a teacher. His reply was discouraging: "*The Western country is a wild country and I would advise no female friend of mine to come to it in any capacity which would bring her into such collision with the natives as you would be as a teacher."* (Capper 1992, 138) Thwarted in that dream of escape, Margaret turned more seriously to writing. Clarke encouraged her to write for the magazine he was starting, *The Western Messenger*, and she translated a Goethe drama for him. She also tried her hand at fiction with a romantic love story. Unfortunately, her fictional characters were too close to life and some of her friends were embarrassed. It would be several years before Margaret tried fiction again.

Margaret's work was disrupted in the fall of 1835 when she fell seriously ill. For nine days and nights, she had a high fever and severe headaches. She may have had typhus (or typhoid) fever, but at the time there was no effective treatment for the disease. Her mother nursed her. Gradually she recovered her strength and when the following Sunday came, her father led family prayers with hearty thanks for Margaret's recovery.

Margaret's siege of illness left the family emotionally drained, but far worse was to come. Within a few days of Margaret's recovery, her father suddenly began to vomit and collapsed on the floor. When the doctor came, he announced that Timothy was suffering from Asiatic cholera. All night Timothy had chills and fever and before the morning of October 1, 1835, he died.

The Fullers were completely unprepared for this devastating blow. Her father, still relatively young and healthy at 57, had left no will. Nor, it turned out, had he left much money for his family. Only by watching every penny would his wife be able to live on her income and pay for the younger children's education. The two older boys, at eighteen and twenty, did not earn enough to help their family. This left Margaret, now twenty-five years old, to take on the responsibility. As an unmarried woman, she could not legally control family property nor have legal authority over her younger brothers and sister. Her uncles, Timothy's brothers, were the only male relatives judged capable of taking charge of the property. Uncle Abraham, her eldest and least sympathetic uncle, was made administrator of the estate.

Margaret was given much of the work of handling the estate and taking care of her family, but she was not allowed to make decisions without consulting her uncle. Nonetheless, being Margaret, she determined to learn as much as she could about business affairs and make sure her family was taken care of as well as possible. The most difficult decision she had to make in the weeks following her father's death was whether to go to Europe with the Farrars. She knew her chances of success as a writer would be better if she went to Europe and met the leading writers there. The well-known American writers of the time, like James Fennimore Cooper and Washington Irving, had spent time abroad. American literature was just beginning to be taken seriously but readers and writers still looked to Europe for models. Traveling with the Farrars would give Margaret a chance to meet important people who might be interested in her work.

On the other hand, who would make sure the younger children and her mother were taken care of if Margaret went away? Uncle Abraham did not value education as Margaret did. Would he be willing to pay for the best schools for the children? Margaret's mother was not strong enough to argue with her brother-in-law. Unhappy though she was to admit it, Margaret knew she would have to stay and take over her father's role in the family.

Margaret's decision was painful, but she was determined to do what she thought was right. She wrote to a friend: *Circumstances have decided that I must not go to Europe, and shut upon me the door, as I think, forever, to the scenes I could have loved. Let me now try to forget myself, and act for others' sakes.* (Fuller and Hudspeth 1983, 1:254)

Chapter 3: Schools and Scandals (1836-1838)

Besides taking care of her family, Margaret needed to earn money. She spent several months after her father's death straightening out his affairs and getting her mother's income established. After that she turned her mind to her own prospects for adding to the family income. She wanted to be a writer, but she needed a job with a regular salary. Teaching was almost the only possibility for an educated woman like Margaret, so she began looking for a school that needed a teacher, but the search took time.

During the summer of 1836 Margaret met Ralph Waldo Emerson, one of the most influential men in the circle of intellectuals living in the Boston/Cambridge area. Emerson, who had given up his post as a Unitarian minister in 1832, was living on his writing as well as a small legacy left him when his young wife, Ellen, died in 1831. He knew many of the same people Margaret knew, and in July 1836, invited her to visit him and his second wife, Lidian, at their Concord home. The visit was not an afternoon call—it lasted three weeks, giving both Emerson and his wife time to learn to know and like Margaret. In his journal Emerson called her "a very accomplished and very intelligent person" (Emerson 1960, 5:188) although years later he wrote of that first meeting that "her talk was a comedy in which dramatic justice was done to everybody's foibles. I remember that she made me laugh more than I liked."

At Emerson's house, Margaret met Bronson Alcott, a philosopher and educational reformer. Many schools in New England at that time were in private homes. An unmarried woman, a widow or a young man just out of college might start a school to earn money. They recruited students from the neighborhood or the families of friends. Teachers had no special training and often gave up teaching as soon as they married or found something that paid better.

Most teachers taught children the same way they had been taught. They expected students to memorize words and sentences and recite them for the teacher. Very few books were available, so children shared simple alphabet books or pages of Bible texts copied by the teacher. Once children learned to read, they struggled with adult books, sounding out the difficult words, sometimes without understanding what they were reading.

Margaret knew the weakness of this method of teaching. She had written in her journal about her own education:

I was now in the hands of teachers, who had not, since they came on the earth, put to themselves one intelligent question as to their business here. Good dispositions and employment for the heart gave a tone to all they said, which was pleasing, and not perverting. They, no doubt, injured those who accepted the husks they proffered for bread, and believed that exercise of memory was study, and to know what others knew, was the object of study. (Fuller, Channing, and Emerson 1857)

Margaret was open to the idea of a different kind of education and was interested in the ideas of Alcott, who was dedicated to an entirely new type of teaching.

Alcott ran one of the most unusual schools in Boston, the Temple School, based on his own philosophy. He believed young children had a natural sense of right and wrong and needed understanding more than instruction. Instead of giving them facts to memorize, he encouraged children to talk and ask questions. Most schools expected students to be silent and listen to the teacher. Perhaps most radical of all, Alcott did not believe in physical punishment.

The size and design of the Temple School set it apart from other schools. Alcott had rented two large, high-ceilinged rooms in a Masonic Temple, one of the most famous buildings in Boston because of the important lectures given there. Large windows let in the daylight, busts of Plato and Jesus were placed on pedestals around the room, and carpets covered the floor. Instead of sitting on long benches as they did in other schools, the children had special desks and chairs. Alcott read the Bible and other books to the children and asked them what they thought about the books. While they talked, his assistant Elizabeth Peabody kept notes on the conversations so they could be published later.

When Elizabeth Peabody resigned her position in the fall of 1836, Margaret had a chance to become Alcott's new assistant. She was curious about Alcott's methods and as she wrote to him, "*I would like to become more conversant with your method of teaching. It would be but an experiment on both sides, for, as I have never yet been subordinate to anyone, I cannot tell how I should please or be pleased. But your proposal has attracted me more than any which has as yet been made to me.*" (Fuller and Hudspeth 1983, 1:256) Alcott hired her to teach French and Latin and to take notes during Alcott's conversations with the children.

For the first few months, everything went well. Margaret had twenty-five pupils including Alcott's daughter, Louisa May Alcott, and her older sister. She loved the children and enjoyed hearing them talk about their thoughts and feelings. Some of the most prominent families in Cambridge and Boston sent their children to the school. Many of the parents had been disappointed in conventional schooling and had high hopes for the experimental education.

Things began to change when Alcott's book, *Conversations with Children about the Gospels*, was published. Conservative critics were shocked that children were being allowed to talk freely about religion instead of being told what to think. As the foreword clearly stated:

It has been a main purpose of the Conductor of these conversations, to tempt forth, by appropriate questions, the cherished sentiments of the children on the subjects presented to their consideration. It was no part of his intention to bring forward, except by necessary implication, his own favorite opinions as a means of biasing, in the smallest degree, the judgments and decisions of the children. (Alcott 1837, xiv).

Some adults were alarmed at the idea of their children being allowed to ask all sorts of questions about Biblical stories instead of being told to accept all of them. Many of the children's comments concerned small points. In discussing the Annunciation, Lemuel said "I do not think Gabriel ought to have told Mary until after John was born, because John came to prepare the way. To which Samuel R. added, "I do not know what was the use of John's coming to announce Jesus. (Alcott 1837,

48). This idle questioning of the Bible stories was bad enough, but Alcott also talked to the children about Jesus' birth and how it happened. This exchange particularly infuriated critics:

Mr. Alcott. And what did you think being born was?

Josiah. It is to take up the body from the earth. The spirit comes from heaven, and takes up the naughtiness out of other people, which makes other people better. And these naughtinesses, put together, make a body for the child; but the spirit is the best part of it. (Alcott 1837, 68)

Alcott hoped for great success with his book, but instead there was a barrage of criticism. Nathan Hale, editor of the Boston Daily Advertiser, attacked Bronson's teaching as an invitation to children to express their "crude and undigested thoughts" upon the most fundamental truths of religion (Baker 1996, 91) and one newspaper suggested that Alcott should be arrested. (Bell 1930, 90-91). Emerson and many other liberal Unitarians defended Alcott, but much of the public was outraged.

One morning while Margaret was teaching, there was a knock on the door. When Alcott opened it, he saw that a mob had gathered. There were shouts of "Down with the Conversations" and "Bring out all your copies and burn them."

Alcott listened calmly, but said nothing. This only infuriated people more. Someone at the back of the crowd shouted "Close the school, dismiss the children and hand over the key."

"No, that I cannot do," answered Alcott.

Through all of this, Margaret tried to continue teaching and to reassure the children that everything would be all right. Finally, young Louisa May Alcott ran out into the entranceway and said to her father, "The children sent me to get you."

Alcott picked up the child and stood there with her in his arms. The mob fell silent for a few seconds. Then Louisa called out, "Go away, bad people!"

For another minute the crowd hesitated then people began to turn and leave. Gradually they all melted away. Alcott closed the door and returned to the classroom. Teaching went on as usual.

Margaret did her best to support Alcott and the school. She had urged him to publish the Conversations and had hoped they would inspire other schools to change. Instead, it was the beginning of the end for the Temple School. Parents began withdrawing their children, and Alcott had to tell Margaret that he could not afford an assistant.

Margaret would have liked to stay and help keep the school going, but she needed to earn a living. Bronson Alcott remained her friend and she kept in touch with what was happening. The school moved from its large rooms into a basement room at the Temple. A few faithful parents kept their children in the school until two years later when Alcott did something too radical even for them.

Many Bostonians were trying to abolish slavery from the Southern United States. Some helped former slaves to escape to freedom in the North or in Canada. Although they hated slavery, they found it difficult to treat former slaves as equals. When Alcott accepted the young daughter of freed slaves as a pupil, parents complained and withdrew their children. Alcott was left with only his own daughters and one other white student to teach. He had no choice but to close the school.

Meanwhile, Margaret moved to Providence, Rhode Island, to teach in another new school. The Greene Street School opened in the fall of 1837 and Margaret was one of its first teachers. Elizabeth Peabody later commented that when she was asked what she would require for a salary, she replied, "How much do you give the Governor of your state? A teacher deserves as much." (Capper 1992, 204) There is no documentation of how much she actually was paid, but Bronson Alcott thought it was very generous.

Hiram Fuller (not related to Margaret), the founder of the school was an admirer of Alcott and wanted his school to be like the Temple School. Classrooms were comfortable and attractive, students were required to keep journals, and physical punishment was not used. Margaret hoped the school would offer the kind of exciting education Alcott had attempted but also include more traditional teaching.

The Greene Street School turned out to be quite different from the Temple School. The students were older, ranging in age from ten to eighteen. They had all come there from more conventional schools where they were expected to listen and memorize rather than to think and talk about their work. They found it difficult to accept the freedom of their new school and were for the most part not interested in discussing their feelings and thoughts about abstract subjects. Margaret was disappointed, especially because even the other teachers cared very little about improving education.

Margaret's teaching load was heavy, but she found time to write to her friends in Boston and to visit them occasionally. Ralph Waldo Emerson, who had become a close friend, was causing a stir among academics and in the liberal community in general. Young people tired of being told they had to follow the rigid rules of their parents' generation crowded his lectures. Emerson encouraged them to think for themselves and decide what kind of work they wanted to do. Fifty years after the American Revolution, he asked for a new revolution in thinking.

The Revolution was still alive in people's memories. Americans were proud of the political independence they had won, but many of them still thought of England as the place where great writers and artists lived. Americans read books written by English authors and wealthy young men went to Europe for a superior education. Emerson and his friends rebelled against this. They believed Americans should break away from European ideas and culture. In a lecture Margaret attended in 1837, Emerson proclaimed, "our long apprenticeship to the learning of other lands, draws to a close." And he concluded, "We will walk on our own feet; we will work with our own hands; we will speak our own minds." (Emerson 1940, 45)

Many older people grumbled that Emerson and his young friends were disrespectful of knowledge that had been passed down through generations. Margaret's father had encouraged her to read stories of ancient Rome. Emerson told her to look into herself for truth and to judge books in the light of her own experience. Unlike many men, Emerson valued women's ideas. He arranged for several women, including Margaret, to attend a meeting of the new Transcendental Club. It was the first time in American history when women were admitted to an important male society. The meeting was a start but the other women gradually stopped coming and the Club soon became a group of men plus Margaret.

Margaret tried many things other women never thought of doing. Women could not vote, so they were not expected to participate in political events, but Margaret did not like being excluded. While she was in Providence, she attended a caucus, a meeting at which the local political party chose its candidate for the coming election. She later wrote to a friend: "I now begin really to feel myself a citizen of the world....I attended last week, somewhat to the horror of Mr.[Hiram] Fuller, the Whig Caucus here....It is rather the best thing I have done." (Higginson 1899, 87) Unlike Emerson and some of the other young rebels, Margaret was not content just to write about exciting new ideas; she was determined to put them into action.

Chapter 4: Moving into a Larger World (1839-1843)

Teaching brought Margaret the money she needed to support herself and contribute to her family, but it didn't satisfy her yearning to be part of the world of ideas. During the years she taught she tried to keep up with the foreign literature being introduced in Boston. Harvard College appointed the émigré scholar Charles Follen its first professor of German and the shortage of European books in the city was alleviated when Elizabeth Peabody opened her bookstore. Faculty and students at Harvard were talking about the exciting new ideas being introduced and Margaret wanted to be part of that excitement.

After two months of intense work when she returned home, she completed the translation of Eckerman's *Conversations with Goethe in the Last Years of His Life*. She sent the manuscript to George Ripley who was editing a series of selections of foreign writers. Margaret's book was published in May and was well received by many Americans who were glad to have access to the great German writer's books. Emerson wrote to her that her work "seems to be a beneficent action for which America will long thank you." (Capper 1992, 254) Eleven years later a British author plagiarized her translation and published it in London where it remained the standard translation of the work for the next century.

Margaret enjoyed the success of her book, but she also had to take care of practical matters. Her mother was finally able to sell the farm in Groton and the family rented a house in Jamaica Plain, only five miles from Boston. Now Margaret was able to attend many concerts and art exhibits in the city. She also spent time with friends, going to parties and visiting their homes for a day or week at a time. Unlike her teenage years when she was lonely and often felt friendless, Margaret's late twenties and thirties were filled with friends. Although she was never described as a great beauty, Margaret had grown into a slim, attractive young woman; her complexion was fair, she moved gracefully and her voice was clear and expressive. Several friends tried to describe what it was about Margaret that captivated people. Perhaps her greatest charm was her deep interest in other people and her sympathy. After only a brief meeting many people found themselves telling her about their lives and problems. She became a guide and mentor to young people as well as a companion to those of her own age.

Emerson later wrote of her:

She wore this circle of friends, when I first knew her, as a necklace of diamonds around her neck....She was everywhere a welcome guest....She stayed a few days, often a week, more seldom a month, and all tasks that could be suspended were put aside to catch the favorable hour, in walking, riding or boating to talk with this joyful guest, who brought wit, anecdotes, love-stories, tragedies, oracles with her...who carried the key to all confidences, and to whom every question had been finally referred. (Fuller, Channing, and Emerson 1857)

Margaret formed many close friendships with women--friendships that would last for the rest of her life. One of her closest friends was Anna Barker, a wealthy young Quaker from New York who frequently visited relatives in Boston. Margaret had known Anna since she was a teenager. As she grew older, Anna became an outstandingly beautiful woman who was admired everywhere she went: in New York, Boston, and New Orleans where her family also had a home.

Margaret also became closer to Sam Ward, a rich, handsome young man who had traveled to Europe and seen many of the paintings and sculpture Margaret admired. They shared an interest in art, literature and ideas and gradually they began to fall in love. Sam worked for his father, who was the American agent for an English bank, so he traveled a great deal. He and Margaret wrote to each other frequently and their relationship developed through letters.

As the spring of 1839 went on, Margaret believed she and Sam Ward were destined to find happiness together. Sam's letters, most of which were later destroyed, were filled with affection and indications of his love. By early summer, however, Margaret found his letters becoming more impersonal. While he was on a long business trip down the Ohio River to New Orleans, she wrote begging to know whether he still cared. It was weeks before she discovered the answer. Sam had visited Anna Barker in New Orleans and decided he loved her. The two became engaged and later married. Margaret remained friendly with both of them, but the shock of losing Sam was painful.

Despite her emotional turmoil, Margaret worked steadily. She still had to earn money to pay some of the costs of educating her younger brothers and sister. How could she put her talents to work in a practical way? Her articles, published in James Freeman Clarke's journal

Western Messenger and Park Benjamin's *American Monthly Magazine* brought her increased reputation as an important intellectual figure, and many people were noticing her gifts.

Emerson and other leaders of the transcendental movement had thought about starting a journal to publish the best work of their group as early as 1835. Emerson would have been the first choice for the post of editor, but he insisted that he needed to spend his time writing and lecturing. Margaret was a young, rising star of the group and her reputation would be burnished by being editor of what the founders hoped would be America's foremost intellectual journal.

Alcott had suggested the new journal be called the *Dial*, which was the name he used for his journals. The group accepted that name and in 1839 they asked Margaret to be the editor; they hoped to bring out the first issue in April 1840.

Margaret had high aspirations for the new journal. She wanted it to present a wide range of topics and wrote:

"I trust there will be a spirit neither of dogmatism nor of compromise, and that this journal will aim, not at leading public opinion, but at stimulating each man to judge for himself, and to think more deeply and more nobly by letting him see how some minds are kept alive by a wise self-trust." (Cooke 1961, 1: 63)

Editing the journal would give Margaret a firm foothold in the intellectual life of Boston, but it was, of course, an unpaid job. There had to be some way to turn her talents to making a living. Eventually she came up with a startling new idea. She would hold a series of conversations for the women of Boston. Women had no opportunity for formal education. All colleges were closed to them. Why couldn't they gather together to discuss the subjects their brothers and husbands studied in college? Under Margaret's direction, they would read and discuss the same serious books that men read.

In the fall of 1839, Margaret sent out a proposal for this series of conversations. The charge was to be ten dollars for a series of thirteen meetings; a high price at the time. By giving two series of conversations a year, Margaret was able to bring in five hundred dollars, an excellent half-time income. Together with her inheritance and the little money she earned by writing, she could support herself. Twenty-five women signed up for the first series, which began on November 6, 1839.

The meetings were held in Elizabeth Peabody's bookstore at 11:00 in the morning. The bookstore was a small space crowded into the front parlor of the Peabody family home, but it was familiar and comfortable for the participants. Margaret would start by introducing a topic and then encourage the women to express their opinions. She aimed high and wanted to discuss important topics, as she wrote to Sophia Ripley, "Could a circle be assembled in earnest, desirous to answer the questions, 'What were we born to do?' and 'How shall we do it?' I should think the undertaking a noble one." (Dall 1895, 5)

Margaret took her conversations very seriously and prepared for them carefully. She dressed the part of a gracious, queenly leader, usually wearing a crimson dress with a white collar to set off her long, graceful neck and neatly pulled-back hair. She used a lorgnette when she glanced at her notes but most often she kept her attention focused on her audience. At first, many women were too shy to speak up, but Margaret usually managed to encourage even the most reluctant. Little by little, they learned to talk more freely about their ideas. In later years many of them remembered Margaret's conversations as the encouragement they needed to become active in speaking out for women's rights.

Several of the women who attended the series kept careful notes of her methods. On one occasion the topic was "What is life?" and the conversation went something like this:

"*Let us define, each in turn, our idea of living. Margaret did not believe we had, any of us, a distinct idea of life.*

"*A.S. thought so great a question ought to be given for a written definition.*

'*No,' said Margaret, 'that is of no use. When we go away to think of anything, we never do think. We all talk of life. We all have some thought now. Let us tell it. C----, what is life?'*

"*C---- replied,--'It is to laugh, or cry, according to our organization.'*

"*'Good,' said Margaret, 'but not grave enough. Come, what is life? I know what I think; I want you to find out what you think.'*

"*Miss P. replied,--'Life is division from one's principle of life in order to a conscious reörganization. We are cut up by time and circumstance, in order to feel our reproduction of the eternal law.'*

"*Mrs. E.,--'We live by the will of God, and the object of life is to submit,' and went on into Calvinism.*

"*Then came up all the antagonisms of Fate and Freedom.*

"*Mrs. H. said,--'God created us in order to have a perfect sympathy from us as free beings.'*

"Mrs. A.B. said she thought the object of life was to attain absolute freedom. At this Margaret immediately and visibly kindled.

"C.S. said,--'God creates from the fulness of life, and cannot but create; he created us to overflow, without being exhausted, because what he created, necessitated new creation. It is not to make us happy, but creation is his happiness and ours.' (Fuller, Channing, and Emerson 1857)

Many women were intoxicated by the opportunity to talk freely and to discuss their ideas and feelings and have them respected. When Margaret broadened the group by inviting some men into it, the women didn't speak up as often, so she returned to women-only conversations and carried them on successfully for five years.

During the early 1840s, Margaret became more involved in social issues. In New England, and especially Boston, new social ideas were bubbling up everywhere. Times were bad for almost everyone. The depression that started in 1837 caused banks to fail and factories to close. Irish immigrants came in large numbers to work as laborers on farms and the new railroads. Because they were so poor, they would work for very low wages, which sometimes meant that other workers lost their jobs. Bitterness grew into violence in some neighborhoods and immigrants were chased out. In rural areas, many farmers had to sell their farms and look for other work.

Aside from economic issues, the major concern of many New Englanders was ending slavery. Most of the men and women Margaret knew thought slavery was wrong but they disagreed about how to end it. Some people thought slave owners should be paid for the loss of their workers, others argued that freed slaves should be sent back to Africa or resettled in the United States. A few people hoped to discourage slavery by refusing to use slave-made goods like cotton clothing. Arguments raged, but neither Margaret nor most of the intellectuals she knew played an active role in the movement for abolition.

Boston was buzzing with discussions about making the world better. Reform schemes became popular and several new communities based on sharing property and work were founded. Margaret knew many of the people involved in experimental community of Brook Farm at West Roxbury, not far from Boston. George Ripley and his wife Sophia started this communal farm where everyone was expected to share the work and benefits of farming. The belief was that if all participated in the less desirable manual labor, each individual would have time for artistic or intellectual work. Emerson and most of the people in his circle visited the community; many gave talks there and observed the way the farm was operating. The Ripleys eagerly encouraged them to join the radical experiment, but few did. Margaret visited the farm several times and discussed social issues with members, but she had little faith in communal life. Like Emerson, she believed that the development of individual character was the key to improving life and society.

Editorial work on the *Dial* took much of Margaret's time. She had to write dozens of letters urging her friends to contribute articles or poetry. She worried whether they would respond, but eventually many of them sent material. The *Dial* never had more than a few hundred readers, but they were important members of the community and were influential in spreading the new ideas coming out of New England.

Chapter 5: Trip to the West (1843)

By 1843, Margaret was firmly established as a leading voice in the intellectual community of Boston. She had written several scholarly articles, edited one of the leading philosophical journals of the day, and translated important German writers. In early spring she finished a long article for the July issue of The *Dial*, "The Great Lawsuit", which she would later expand into her most famous book *Women in the Nineteenth Century*. In it she wrote the ringing challenge, "We would have every arbitrary barrier thrown down. We would have every path laid open to women as freely as to men." She was ready to lay aside her pen for a while and turn to fresh experiences.

So far most of her intellectual discoveries had come through books and conversations. She had scarcely seen anything of America beyond New England. She longed to go to Europe to learn more about the exciting new ideas and movements there, but she didn't have enough money to go there. When her friend James Freeman Clarke and his sister Sarah Ann Clarke suggested she travel with them to some of the new Western States, Margaret knew the opportunity was too good to miss. The Clarkes had a brother who had settled in Chicago and a trip to visit him would give the party a chance to see the frontier areas around the Great Lakes.

Money was still scarce, but a friend, Sarah Shaw, unexpectedly paid Margaret generously in exchange for language lessons Margaret had given her. This payment, plus some help from the Clarkes, meant that money would not be a problem during the trip.

The trip would take the group through Michigan, which become a state six years earlier and to the western border of the United States at the edge of the Wisconsin and Iowa territories.

The group traveled from Boston to New York by coach and took a train to Albany and then Buffalo and the nearby Niagara Falls. Margaret was not as impressed by the falls as she had hoped, perhaps because she had seen many paintings of them and knew just what to expect. On the other hand, the turbulent rapids in the Niagara River, which she saw when she walked across a bridge to Goat Island, were a surprise. She wrote: "The rapids enchanted me far beyond what I expected; they are so swift that they cease to seem so; you can think only of their beauty." (Fuller 1991, 5) Margaret was amused by the tourists, who had already begun flocking to the falls. She described one man who "walked close up to the fall, and, after looking at it for a moment, with an air as if thinking how he could best appropriate it to his own use, he spat into it." (Fuller 1991, 5).

Continuing their trip, the three friends took a steamboat from Niagara to begin a circular tour of the Great Lakes traveling sometimes by boat and sometimes on a coach or wagon through the interior of Wisconsin and Michigan. They went as far north as Mackinac Island, as far west as Milwaukee, south to Pawpaw, Illinois, and then back to Buffalo. It was a long and sometimes dangerous trip through country that was only sparsely settled.

Margaret kept a journal of her impressions, which she hoped to turn into articles when she returned home. She was eager to see for herself the lives of the western settlers and also to document the plight of the local Indian tribes. Like Emerson and other friends, she had been shocked by the Indian Removal Policy pursued by Presidents Andrew Jackson and Martin Van Buren whereby Indian tribes were pushed out of the Eastern states and into areas west of the Mississippi River. Although the policy was not followed as rigorously in the North as in the Southern states, many of the Great Lakes tribes in southern Michigan, Ohio, Indiana, and Illinois were forced to leave their homes for new lands in Kansas and Oklahoma. In Wisconsin, the United States failed to completely remove any of the tribes. Most of the Potawatomi, Ojibwa, and Ottawa who lived in southern Wisconsin were removed to Kansas in the 1830s, but some Potawatomi refused to go and instead moved to northern Wisconsin.

Margaret was keenly aware of how recently the Indians had lived on the lands she traveled through. As she passed through Oregon, Illinois, along the banks of the Rock River, she mused: *How happy the Indians must have been here. It is not long since they were driven away and the ground, above and below, is full of their traces.....You have only to turn up the sod to find arrowheads and Indian pottery. On an island, belonging to our host, and nearly opposite his house, they loved to stay. And, no doubt, enjoyed its lavish beauty as much as the myriad wild pigeons that now haunt its flower filled shades.* (Fuller 1991, 32-33)

She had never seen anything as awe inspiring as the dense forests of oak and tamarack trees along the upper reaches of the Great Lakes. Like her friends

Emerson and Thoreau she was fascinated by the natural world and impressed by the wilderness of the Northwest Territories. She also paid attention to the way people lived in the West compared with New England. She found that most women had a difficult time adjusting to life in the West.

The great drawback upon the lives of these settlers, at present, is the unfitness of the women for their new lot. It has generally been the choice of the men, and the women follow, as women will...but too often in heartsickness and weariness....their part is the hardest, and they are least fitted for it....The women can rarely find any aid in domestic labor. All its various and careful tasks must often be performed, sick or well, by the mother and daughters, to whom a city education has imparted neither the strength nor skill now demanded. (Fuller 1991, 38)

Margaret was practical enough to realize that if Eastern families did not accept changes in their lifestyles they would never be happy in the West. She noticed that the pianos many settlers had carried all the way out to Illinois and Wisconsin became useless in a few years. The women did not have time to practice and keep up their skill. To make things worse, the damp weather caused the pianos to go out of tune quickly and no piano tuners were available. Women wanted their children to learn to play, but were unable to tune pianos themselves. *"The guitar or some portable instrument,"* she wrote *"which requires less practice, and could be kept in tune by themselves, would be far more desirable for most of these ladies It would give all they want as a household companion to fill up the gaps of life with pleasant stimulus or solace, and be sufficient accompaniment to the voice in social meetings."* (Fuller 1991, 40)

The plight of European immigrants who bought cheap land in the states of the Northwest Territory also stirred her sympathy. Even more than families from the Eastern United States, the Swedes, Norwegians, and Irish who tried to become farmers suffered in the harsh unaccustomed climate. The hard physical labor required to clear the land as well as the lack of doctors, schools, and the amenities of European life were shocks some of them never overcame.

Margaret spent the final week of her trip visiting Mackinac Island off the shore of Michigan. She was eager to see a gathering of Chippewa and Ottawa Indians, almost two thousand of them, who were going to the island to collect their annual payment from the United States government for the land they had given up. During her years in New England, Margaret had been aware of the injustice in the treatment of Indians, but she had not seen it at first hand. Her journey through the West gave her an opportunity to see Indian settlements for herself. She wrote to her brother Richard, "It is only five years since the poor Indians have been dispossessed of this region of sumptuous loveliness, such as can hardly be paralleled in this world. No wonder they poured out their blood freely before they would go." (Fuller and Hudspeth 1983, 3:132)

From her hotel window on Mackinac Island, Margaret could see on the curving beach clusters of Indian lodges *"with their amber brown matting, so soft, and bright of hue, in the late afternoon sun….The Indians were grouped and scattered among the lodges; the women preparing food, in the kettle or frying pan…the children, half-naked, wild as little goblins, were playing both in and out of the water."*

(Fuller 1991, 107) Margaret enjoyed walking through the Indian encampments, communicating with the women through signs. She was struck by the gentleness of the men with their children and by the way they enjoyed sitting around the campfire telling stories.

Margaret liked to walk among the Indians and observe their actions, but she was aware that most white settlers had only contempt for them. "*[W]ith white women it seems to amount to disgust, to loathing. How I could endure the dirt, the peculiar smell of the Indians, and their dwellings was a great marvel in the eyes of my lady acquaintance; indeed I wonder why they did not quite give me up, as they certainly looked on me with great distaste for it.*" (Fuller 1991, 113)

There seemed no way to bring the two races together in peace. The Chippewa had petitioned the governor of Michigan to admit them as citizens, but Margaret did not think this would solve the problem "unless they could be admitted as brothers, to the heart of the white man". And that did not seem possible while white people were so sure of their superiority. She considered amalgamation of races a solution that "would afford the only true and profound means of civilization" but dismissed that as unlikely. In the end it appeared the Indians were "fated to perish". (Fuller 1991, 120) She left Mackinac Island with a profound sense of sorrow.

During her trip to Mackinac Island, Margaret seized the opportunity to take a steamer to Sault Sainte Marie where she stayed overnight. In the morning she hired two guides to take her in a canoe to shoot down the rapids and was thrilled with the speed and danger of the trip. That was the last adventure of her trip. Margaret and the Clarkes started home on a steamboat, stopping briefly at Detroit, and then back to Buffalo where the Clarkes stayed while Margaret took the train to Albany and a river steamboat down to New York.

The trip had been a long one and Margaret was tired from the journey and the press of new impressions. She had written to Emerson from Chicago,

O what can be so forlorn in its forlorn parts as this travelling? The ceaseless packing and unpacking, the heartless, uncongenial intercourses, the cheerless hotel, the many hours when you are too tired and your feelings too much dissipated to settle to any pursuit, yet you either have nothing to look at or are weary of looking. And she was both attracted and repelled by the life she had seen in the West. She continued: *Truly there is no place for me to live, I mean as regards being with men. I like not the petty intellectualities, cant, and bloodless theory there at home, but this merely instinctive existence, to those who live it so 'first rate' 'off hand' and 'go ahead', pleases me no better.* (Fuller and Hudspeth 1983, 3:143)

In New York, Margaret had little time to sort through her impressions of the trip. She soon met some of her old friends from Boston. William Channing took her to his church in the city where she ran into Henry Thoreau as well as Bronson Alcott, who was trying to raise money for Fruitlands, a radical community he was starting. She went to Staten Island to see Emerson's brother, William, who had settled there to practice law and also received two visits from Henry James Sr., whose sons William and Henry were infants. Finally she headed back to New England.

Among the first people Margaret visited after her return were Emerson and his wife Lidian. She entertained them with stories of her travels and her impressions of the people she had met and the places she visited. Emerson urged her to write a book about her trip and she agreed to try. When she went to her journals and notes, she was disappointed to find how many details were missing. In her haste to write about the events of each day she had neglected to describe the place she had seen and even the names of some of the lakes and rivers they had seen. Fortunately, Sarah Clarke had made many sketches of their travels, which she turned into engravings, and Margaret was able to use those as illustrations. She was so eager to find more details about the exploration of Indian territories that she requested and received permission to use the Harvard College Library. Students visiting the library that fall were surprised to see a lone female among the readers; Margaret was the first woman who had ever been allowed to use the college library.

Margaret worked hard on her book interrupted only by the Conversations which she continued to hold because she needed the income. She refused to write any reviews for the *Dial* and gave up her idea of translating more Goethe pieces until the book was finished. By May of 1844, she finally had a completed manuscript and turned to Emerson for advice about publishing it. He handled all the details of publication and the Boston publishers Little and Brown brought out the first edition in the summer of 1844. The book was an immediate success and Margaret wrote to William Channing that it was "much read and esteemed 'very entertaining'."

Margaret's trip to the Great Lakes led not only to her first published book, *Summer on the Lakes* in 1843; it also changed Margaret and broadened her vision. Although she was still very much a New Englander, she had seen a new type of American and became aware of a world beyond transcendentalism and Harvard intellectuals. She was not eager to return to what now seemed their rather self-satisfied provincial life. She began to feel that Emerson's focus on self-cultivation and her own earlier concentration on interior wisdom should lead to action. Her conscience was aroused by the plight of the Indians and she would become increasingly concerned with other people who were being treated badly. She was ready to leave the world she had grown up in and move on to new scenes and new endeavors.

Chapter 6: New York Journalist (1844-46)

The publication of Margaret's book, *Summer on the Lakes*, made her name known outside of Boston but did not bring in enough money to live on for long. Her Conversations were still successful, but the audience was small and she could not consider them a permanent career. She was determined not to return to teaching, one of the few reliable professions for women. Her severe headaches made it difficult for her to follow a fixed schedule, so she preferred writing, which she could work on when she felt well but postpone when headaches came. Besides, writing would be taken seriously even by men. Editing the *Dial* magazine had brought her into contact with most of the intellectuals in New England, but she wanted time to do her own work. She also wanted to expand her life to include more than just endless work; she watched her friends form attachments and get married and she longed for an emotional life of her own.

In 1844, help came from a surprising source. Her Conversations has attracted Molly Greeley, wife of the Horace Greeley a journalist who had recently founded The *Tribune* in New York City. Molly sat in on some of the conversations during her visits to Boston and, impressed by Margaret's insights, she suggested to her husband that he invite Margaret to write for the *Tribune*. After reading "The Great Lawsuit" and some of Margaret's other essays in the *Dial*, he decided to offer Margaret a position, which she was glad to accept.

Shortly before leaving Massachusetts, Margaret had finished writing a book based in part on her article "The Great Lawsuit" which she had published in the *Dial*. This new book *Women in the Nineteenth Century* would be the basis for much of her later fame — and infamy. Her book called for nothing less than the perfection of man, and as she specified, *By Man I mean both man and woman: these are the two halves of one thought. I lay no especial stress on the welfare of either. I believe that the development of the one cannot be effected without that of the other.* (Fuller M., A. Fuller and Rosenthal, 1971,1) She was, however, aware that even in America men have had a greater opportunity to raise themselves: *As men become aware that few men have had a fair chance, they are inclined to say that no women have had a fair chance.* (Fuller M., A. Fuller and Rosenthal, 1971, 8)

Drawing on her knowledge of myth, history, and philosophy she gave many examples of the roles women have played throughout history and argued that women should view themselves and be treated as autonomous individuals, not only as wives and mothers. She envisioned men and women as equals and partners. One sentence in the book would be more closely associated with her than anything else she ever wrote:

But if you ask me what offices they [women] may fill, I reply — any. I do not care what case you put; let them be sea captains, if you will. I do not doubt there are women well fitted for such an office... (Fuller M., A. Fuller and Rosenthal, 1971, 95)

Margaret knew from personal experience that girls and women had many different talents and interests. She sounded very modern when she wrote:

In families that I know some little girls like to saw wood, others to use carpenter's tools. Where these tastes are indulged, cheerfulness and good humor are promoted. Where they are forbidden, because 'such things are not proper for girls' they grow sullen and mischievous. (Fuller M., A. Fuller and Rosenthal, 1971, 95)

Margaret's book questions the prevalent belief that women should devote themselves solely to domestic affairs, while their husbands control the family. Husbands at that time could take children away from their wives or threaten to do so whenever their wives questioned their authority. Women whose husbands died without making a will were not allowed to assume the status of head of the family but were treated as little more than a child, inheriting only a portion of the family fortune even if they had brought money or property to the marriage. Margaret argued that having influence inside the home was not sufficient for equality because men could not fairly represent women when *"not one man ...in the hundred million can rise above the belief that woman was made for man."* (Fuller M., A. Fuller and Rosenthal, 1971, 15)

Although it was daring for an unmarried woman like Margaret to write about equality in marriage, she went even further in discussing sexual equality. She pointed to the existence of prostitutes as further evidence that the inequality between men and women led naturally to the exploitation of some women. She decried the acceptance of prostitution, writing *"where legislators admit that ten thousand prostitutes are a fair proportion to one city, and husbands tell wives it is folly to expect chastity from men, it is inevitable that there should be many monsters of vice."* (Fuller M., A. Fuller and Rosenthal, 1971, 80)

The book ended with a plea that women be allowed to develop themselves fully as individuals so they could join in marriage as equal partners rather than dependents and followers. *"It is a vulgar error that love, a love, to women is her whole existence; she also is born for Truth and Love in their universal energy."* (Fuller M., A. Fuller and Rosenthal, 1971, 97)

Horace Greeley published *Women in the Nineteenth Century* and sold the entire edition of 1500 books within a week. Margaret was delighted, having expected that only a thousand or so would sell in the first two years. She earned the satisfying amount of $85 and was even happy when the book was pirated and published in England. The publication brought a flurry of attention to Margaret who was praised by many in the press. The liberal newspapers were pleased, of course, and even some conservatives who did not share Margaret's politics praised her courage in writing it. The *Charleston Mercury* called it "the first work that has taken the liberal side in the question of Women's Rights since Mary Wollstonecraft." (Capper 2007, 188) Not all writers approved, of course, the *Southern Quarterly Review* thought that in calling for women's equality Margaret was urging women to give up their greatest strength — the weakness that was their real power. Edgar Allen Poe wrote that Margaret "judges women by the heart and intellect of Miss Fuller, but there are not more than one or two Miss Fullers on the whole face of the earth" (Chevigny 1976, 233)

In Boston, opinion was mixed. Lydia Maria Child, the most prominent of the anti-slavery writers, called it a "bold book" and thought Margaret courageous for having said many things that needed to be said. Sophia Hawthorne, on the other hand, objected to its portrait of men. She wrote: "The impression it left was disagreeable. I did not like the tone of it — & did not agree with her at all about the change in woman's outward circumstances ... Neither do I believe in such a character of man as she gives. It is altogether too ignoble ... I think Margaret speaks of many things that should not be spoken of." (Miller 1991, 235). Emerson, who had declined to write a preface for the book, was noncommittal. He had already told her in speaking about women's rights that "only in poetic form could this right and wrong be portrayed" (Capper 2007, 187), so he was probably uncomfortable with Margaret's frank discussion of sexual politics and prostitution. Margaret relished the attention being given the book, although she was disappointed in the reactions of some of her friends. She wrote to her brother Richard: "here as often before I have found the stranger more sympathizing and in my belief intelligent than some of my private friends." (Fuller and Hudspeth 1983, 4:64)

Moving to New York City was a dramatic change for Margaret. Boston, although a major business center, was an older, quieter city than New York, which was already famous for its forward-looking spirit. New York had the largest and busiest harbor in the world. The completion of the Erie Canal in the 1820s had given the city a great advantage over Boston and Philadelphia because it could send goods directly to the growing Midwest. Shipping and commerce from Europe and the Southern United States started flowing through New York, which in turn led to an influx of workers and immigrants from many countries and cultures. When the canal was completed in 1825, New York was a city of 166,000 and did not extend further north than 14th Street, by 1840 the population had grown to 312,000. It was more than three times the size of Boston and far larger than any other city in the United States. The streets were crowded with horses pulling wagons and carts. Pedestrians had to skitter around steaming horse dung and avoid heavy barrels being rolled through the streets by sweaty workmen shouting warnings in incomprehensible languages. It was very different from the quiet green lawns of Harvard College.

The city's cosmopolitan attitude and tolerance of many different cultures encouraged immigrant groups to settle in the city. Already some people regarded New York as a strange, almost foreign, city. Edgar Allan Poe, who moved to New York in the same year that Margaret did, saw the immigrants as an amusing alien intrusion into American life. In describing the city soon after his arrival, he included their homes with the landscape:

Trees are few; but some of the shrubbery is exceedingly picturesque. Not less so are the prevalent shanties of the Irish squatters. I have one of these tabernacles (I use the term primitively) at present in the eye of my mind. It is, perhaps, nine feet by six, with a pigsty applied externally, by way both of portico and support. The whole fabric (which is of mud) has been erected in somewhat too obvious an imitation of the Tower of Pisa. A dozen rough planks, "pitched" together, form the roof. The door is a barrel on end. There is a garden, too; and this is encircled by a ditch at one point, a large stone at another, a bramble at a third. A dog and a cat are inevitable in these habitations; and, apparently, there are no dogs and no cats more entirely happy. (Poe 1846)

Horace Greeley was an ambitious young man from New Hampshire, a year younger than Margaret, who had left school at 14 to become a printer. To advance his career, he moved to New York where he became a contributor to periodicals supporting the Whig party. In 1841, he started a new paper, the *Tribune*, as a competitor to the twelve other newspapers then operating in the city. He intended the *Tribune* to be an innovative American newspaper that would offer objective news stories on many subjects rather than be the voice of one political party as most of the other papers were. Greeley supported many liberal causes including temperance and women's rights as well as the abolition of slavery. His wife, Mary Cheney Greeley, believed in women's suffrage and spiritualism as well as healthy eating. She was a follower of Sylvester Graham (inventor of graham crackers), the dietary reformer who advocated a vegetarian diet based on whole grain bread as a means of combating alcoholism and lust. Mary was interested in the arts and culture and struggled with the practicalities of running a home. While her husband went downtown to his office and his newspaper, she suffered through the loss of two infants and tried to keep house while maintaining her lofty principles. Some unfriendly critics suggested that the plain vegetarian food served in the Greeley household led Horace to eat most of his meals at restaurants near his downtown office.

The Greeleys had bought a farm in what was then a rural part of New York City overlooking Turtle Bay on the East River. They were close to what is now 49th Street, but the populated part of the city itself still ended at 14th Street. The area around Turtle Bay was largely rural with green fields and woods dotted by a few houses. The road, about a quarter mile from their house offered transportation downtown by horse and carriage. The Greeleys told Margaret they would provide a room for her so she would not have to look for housing in New York.

Margaret traveled to New York in November 1844 and moved into the Greeley home, where she had a large bedroom overlooking the East River. Horace Greeley went to the office early every day and often worked late, but Margaret usually worked at home writing book reviews and articles about social conditions in the city. Describing her setting to her brother Eugene, she wrote:

As to a home, the place where we live is old and dilapidated, but in a situation of great natural loveliness. When there I am perfectly secluded, yet everyone I wish to see comes to see me and I can get to the center of the city in half an hour....I do just as I please, and as much or little as I please, and the editors express themselves perfectly satisfied. (Fuller and Hudspeth 1983, 4:56)

Despite the cheerful view she sent to her brother, Margaret did not always find life at the Greeleys easy. Molly was dissatisfied with her husband's long hours away in the city and distressed over the loss of their two infants. She spent much of her time complaining about her health and embracing reforms that might make her and the world better. A strong opponent of animal cruelty, she once embarrassed Margaret when she met her in the city wearing kid gloves by shrieking, "Skin of a beast! Skin of a beast!" Shocked, Margaret reacted by asking, "What do you wear?" and when Molly answered

"Silk" Margaret shouted "Entrails of a worm!" (Seitz 1926, 331).

Because New York was larger than Boston, Margaret could attend more concerts and plays; she also went to parties in the home of her old friend Lydia Maria Child, a well-known novelist and abolitionist, where she met writers and radicals and learned about political activities in the city. The anti-slavery activist Cassius M. Clay gave thrilling lectures describing the destruction of his printing press by an angry mob in Kentucky. European revolutionists brought news about the movement to unite the many states of Italy. And the elderly Quaker Isaac Hopper talked about his controversial plan to start the first halfway house for female convicts, although most people still believed such women should be hidden away and shunned by all god-fearing citizens.

Margaret had been hired to write theater and book reviews, but Greeley also asked her to comment on social conditions. He believed that as a woman Margaret would have a distinctive and sympathetic view of city life. Most Americans lived in small towns or rural areas and the problems arising from the crowding and fast growth of a large city were new to them. Many did not know that despite being a successful business center and home to wealthy people, New York suffered from high rates of poverty, crime, and illness.

From the window of her bedroom at the Greeley's house, Margaret could see Blackwell Island in the East River, which housed a large prison for women, an insane asylum, and charity hospital wards. No group of people aroused Margaret's sympathy more than the women prisoners she visited at Blackwell Penitentiary.

Margaret understood that most of the prisoners were prostitutes and, as she wrote in a letter, "I have always felt great interest in these women, who are trampled in the mud to gratify the brute appetites of men." (Capper 2007, 207) She was shocked by what she saw at the prison and wrote:

Passing to the Penitentiary we entered on one of the gloomiest scenes that deforms the great metropolis. Here are the twelve hundred, who receive the punishment....And under what circumstances! Never was punishment treated more simply as a social convenience, without regard to pure right, or a hope of reformation.... (Fuller and Kelley 1994, 374).

There were no matrons to supervise the prisoners' care and the male guards were unsympathetic. Margaret believed women should care for women prisoners. She urged that prisoners be separated so those who had committed minor crimes would not be corrupted by more hardened criminals.

At the Asylum for the Insane Margaret noticed, and reported to her readers, that twice as many people were crowded into the building as could be accommodated. As a result, patients sat on the floor, scarcely talked, and seemed isolated from everything around them. "Here," she wrote of the city hospital on Blackwell Island, "insanity appeared in its more stupid, wild, or despairing forms. They crouched in corners; they had no eye for the stranger, no heart for hope, no habitual expectation of light." (Fuller, Bean and Myerson 2000, 101) She contrasted this with the Bloomingdale Institute a model facility run by the New York Hospital and suggested that more individual attention should be paid to each patient. Margaret's comments sound modern because she recognized the importance of treating mentally troubled people as members of the community. The changes she suggested were not put into practice until many years later, but she was among the first people in America to write about treatment for the mentally ill.

In all of the institutions she visited, Margaret observed carefully and suggested to her readers the steps that they as citizens might take to help the situation.

The recognized principles of all such institutions which have any higher object than the punishment of fault, (and we believe few among us are so ignorant as to avow that as the only object, though they may, from want of thought, act as if it were,) are – Classification as the first step, that the bad may not impede those who wish to do well; 2d. Instruction, practical, oral, and by furnishing books which may open entirely new hopes and thoughts to minds oftener darkened than corrupted; 3d. A good Sanitary system, which promotes self-respect, and through health and purity of body, the same in mind. (Fuller, Bean and Myerson 2000, 102)

Another group of people in the city who were ignored by many of her readers were the immigrants. Thousands of poor people, many of them Irish immigrants who had fled the poverty of the old country lived in New York. Most had little education and would take any job as a laborer or servant. Native-born workers resented the newcomers, especially because they were Roman Catholics, which seemed to some Protestants a dangerous and alien religion. In New York as well as several other large cities, there were anti-Irish riots during the 1840s. Some employers put up notices reading "No Irish need apply" when they advertised for workers.

Margaret was more understanding than her readers when she wrote about immigrants:

They are looked upon with contempt for their want of aptitude in learning new things; their ready and ingenious lying; their eye service. These are the faults of an oppressed race, which must require the aid of better circumstances through two or three generations to eradicate. Their virtues are their own;--they are many, genuine, and deeply rooted. Can an impartial observer fail to admire their truth to domestic ties, their power of generous bounty and more generous gratitude, their indefatigable good humor, (for ages of wrong, which have driven them to so many acts of desperation, could never sour their blood at its source) their ready wit, their elasticity of nature. They are at bottom one of the best nations of the world,--Would they were welcomed here, not to work merely, but to intelligent sympathy and efforts, both patient and ardent for the education of their children. (Fuller, Bean and Myerson 2000. 148)

This article on "The Irish Character" brought angry objections from some readers who believed the Irish, and all immigrants, were a threat to American society, but Margaret continued to speak up for people she considered mistreated. Her social commentary became as important for her as the literary criticism she was writing.

Meanwhile she was also enjoying the energy and drive of the people she knew in New York. Years later Caroline Sturgis said to Emerson, "The persons she knew best were more vehement, adventurous, and various than her friends here [Boston]; less moral, less poetical, less beautiful than some she had known, but she enjoyed their freedom from the Puritanism that had annoyed her here." (Capper 2007, 220) One of the most exciting, and perhaps less moral, friends she made in New York was James Nathan a Jewish immigrant from Germany who was almost the same age as she was and had moved to the city from Hamburg fifteen years earlier. She met him at a New Year's Eve party and soon began seeing him frequently. He was a handsome man with a "rich, persuasive" voice and an interest in the art and culture that Margaret enjoyed.

Nathan took her to concerts and plays. Together they heard the violinist Ole Bull play on his Stradivarius; they took long walks through the woods near the Greeley house and talked about his ambitions to be a writer. Soon they were writing letters to each other almost every day. Their friendship flourished through letters and outings, but Margaret did not tell her friends about their growing intimacy. Mary Greeley was a difficult woman, and often jealous of Margaret's many friends, so perhaps it was natural for Margaret to avoid bringing Nathan to their house. Rebecca and Marcus Spring, two other close friends, also appeared to be vaguely suspicious of Nathan and to think he was using Margaret to gain access to people who would not otherwise know him. There were many Jews in New York at the time, but most of them lived in a few Jewish neighborhoods and did not often socialize with other groups. Anti-Semitism was common among Christians, but Margaret, unlike some of her friends, was fascinated by Nathan's background and experiences. Being both Jewish and in the clothing business, made him seem exotic in the intellectual Unitarian circle of Margaret's friends. Discretion about their close friendship seemed to be a wise course.

Nathan may have had his own reasons for keeping the relationship quiet. His letters to Margaret have disappeared, but from her answers it seems he confessed to her some past indiscretions. Her letters contain tantalizing hints: "*Indeed I have suffered much since receiving the letter….I felt the falsity of the position in which you had placed yourself, that you had acted a fiction and though from honorable…motives had entered the path of intrigue….I do not see my friend, how you can feel thus secure against this being generally known.*" (Fuller and Hudspeth 1983, 4:69) To the modern reader, Margaret's words seem deliberately obscure, but no doubt Nathan understood what she meant. There were rumors that he was living with an English woman who had followed him to New York after an affair in London. Whether these were true or not, and how much Margaret knew, has never been determined.

Margaret certainly thought, at least for a while, that she had found someone to whom she could confide her deepest feelings. Her emotions were stirred and she longed to see Nathan more often. One day in May she wrote to him:

The Editor is gone away till Sunday and the evenings are open to music. Will you not come to-morrow evening? You know there was to be one with the guitar and there may not be such another free opportunity. (Fuller and Gotendorf 1903, 65)

But Nathan did not come that evening and many other evenings she waited for him in vain. At some time in the early summer of 1845, Nathan surprised Margaret by telling her he was leaving New York for an extended trip to England, Germany and the Middle East.

The correspondence continued while Nathan was in Europe. Margaret wrote long letters describing what she was doing and reminiscing about what they had done together.

I do not now go out in the afternoon or evening, which was the time we used to be together, but choose the morning rather. I have got a new place on the rocks which is delightful in the morning, much more so than the one where we used to go; it is more shadowed and retired; yet the water comes up to my feet. But you, I fear, will never see it. (Fuller and Gotendorf 1903, 111)

There is no record of how often Nathan replied to Margaret or how much he told her about his life during those months in Europe, but he was still the center of much of her emotional life

Margaret's family and early biographers struggled to keep any mention of Nathan out of the records of her life. They preferred to think of Margaret as immune from the ordinary emotions of less intellectual women. It was not until 1873 that Nathan, who had changed his name to Gotendorf and was living in Germany, decided to publish Margaret's letters. When *Love Letters of Margaret Fuller* appeared, many of Margaret's friends and family were appalled, although the letters are neither scandalous nor revealing. They show the two had a close friendship, and that at least for a while she had hoped their relationship might last for a lifetime.

Margaret's intense interest in Nathan did not prevent her from keeping up with her work on the *Tribune*. She continued writing reviews of books and articles as well as social commentary, but her time in New York only increased her yearning to travel even further and she began looking for an opportunity to go to Europe. When Horace Greeley agreed that she could become the European correspondent for the *Tribune*, she was jubilant. Her life was expanding in ever-widening circles and she looked forward to the future.

Chapter 7: Europe at Last (1846-1847)

America in the 1840s was a young, uncertain society that looked upon Europe as the home of true culture. Like most Americans, Margaret had never seen the famous art she had read about in books. Her only knowledge of the paintings of Raphael and the statues of Michelangelo were copies made by visiting Americans or black-and-white prints in books. None of these gave anything like the experience of viewing originals.

In 1846, Margaret traveled to Europe with two friends, Marcus and Rebecca Spring, a Quaker couple she had met in New York. Marcus was a wealthy cotton merchant who had broken away from the Society of Friends to work with more liberal Unitarian groups on antislavery and social reform campaigns. His wife, Rebecca, grew up in a strongly antislavery family; her father was the first president of the New England Antislavery Society. The Springs socialized in the same circles as Margaret and she spent many weekends at Rose Cottage, their large house in Brooklyn.

The Springs offered to pay the fare for Margaret's trip in return for her tutoring their twelve-year-old son, Edward. Margaret got along well with children and both she and Edward looked forward to being teacher and student on the trip. To cover her additional expenses, she would write news reports for Greeley's *Tribune*.

There was a flurry of activity as Margaret packed up her belongings in New York and took them with her on the rail trip to Boston where she would store her things with her mother. After a few hurried farewells to her Boston friends and to her family, she was ready to leave with the Springs on August 1. They sailed on the maiden voyage of the British Cunard steamer Cambria to Liverpool. They were lucky in the ship they chose. Unlike Emerson, who had traveled to England thirteen years earlier and had to sleep in large dormitory-style accommodations, the Cambria had comfortable cabins for its passengers. The increasing number of trans-Atlantic travelers made it worthwhile for steamship companies to offer far more amenities than they had ever provided before.

The journey was a very quick one of only ten days, a record for the times, but for Margaret it was still too long. The passengers had to listen to the constant grinding of the paddles and endure the dark black smoke trailing from the smokestacks and the sickening smell of its engine oil. When they finally reached England, Margaret wrote to her mother, "I enjoyed nothing on the sea; the excessively bracing air so affected me that I could not bear to look at it. The sight of land delighted me." Despite the short trip, she wrote, "I did not complain, but I could hardly have borne another day." (Fuller and Hudspeth 1983, 4:225)

The Cambria sailed to Liverpool where the passengers disembarked and Margaret had her first view of England. The Liverpool docks extended for miles on either side of their landing, far larger and more crowded than any docks in America. It was an impressive sight. On the day after their arrival, the group went to Manchester only 27 miles away and it was there that Margaret had a chance to see more of English life.

In Manchester, Margaret and the Springs visited the Mechanics Institute where they saw boys and young men in their classes and Margaret was pleased to find that the Institute had recently admitted girls and women to their programs. In contrast to these educational efforts, Margaret observed other less edifying sights in England and wrote of how she and her friends were "compelled to turn a deaf ear to the squalid and shameless beggars of Liverpool, or talking by night in the streets of Manchester to the girls from the Mills who were strolling bare-headed, with coarse, rude and reckless air through the streets, seeing through the windows of its gin-palaces the women seated drinking, too dull to carouse." (Fuller, Reynolds and Smith 1991, 47) Even in the beautiful countryside she saw "swarms of dirty women and dirtier children at the doors of the cottages" and she worried about the "frightful inequalities between the lot of man and man" (Fuller, Reynolds and Smith 1991, 72).

The group went from Liverpool to Scotland, traveling by coach, train and canal boat. Margaret did not like the railroads. Traveling by railroad, she wrote is "the most stupid process on earth; …the noise of the train makes it impossible either to read, talk, or sleep to advantage" (Fuller, Reynolds and Smith 1991. 69). She preferred gliding on a canal boat pulled by horses through a quiet landscape past the lawns of large country houses. On the canal, she and her friends could admire the houses and gardens and talk comfortably with other travelers.

Margaret was looking forward to receiving a letter from James Nathan, and she found one waiting in Edinburgh. Nathan wrote to tell Margaret he had become engaged to marry a German woman. Margaret's pride was deeply hurt by this unexpected blow. She had hoped the misunderstandings of their last few weeks in New York would disappear during their separation. Instead, all her dreams of a lifelong friendship, and perhaps romance, were shattered. Without telling Rebecca and Marcus what Nathan had written, she destroyed the letter and resolved to carry on as though nothing had happened.

After a few days of sightseeing in Edinburgh, which Margaret called a "beautiful and stately city" the group left for three weeks of travel through the Highlands of Scotland. Margaret enjoyed traveling by stagecoach through the hilly countryside, and the visit to the ruined castle where Mary Queen of Scots had lived. The mists and chilly winds in Scotland did not dim Margaret's enthusiasm for the countryside and when Marcus Spring proposed that she walk up Ben Lomond, the highest mountain in the area, with him, she accepted eagerly. The two of them set out on the four-mile climb to the summit while Rebecca stayed below with young Eddie. It was a clear day, so they did not bother to take a guide. When they reached the highest peak they were thrilled. "Peak beyond peak caught from the shifting light all the colors of the prism, and on the farthest angel companies seemed hovering in their glorious white robes," wrote Margaret (Fuller, Reynolds and Smith 1991, 74).

About four o'clock in the afternoon the two weary but exhilarated hikers started back down the mountain. The trail was not clearly marked and they accidentally strayed from it. After trying in vain to find the path down to their inn, Marcus left Margaret to rest while he went off to search for it by himself. When he did not return after ten minutes, she became alarmed and called him several times but got no answer. The evening was coming on, so finally she started down the mountain on her own.

As she scrambled down the boggy hillside, Margaret's feet became wet and the skirts of her long dress were soon water-soaked and heavy. With every step, the soggy fabric slapped against her legs and chilly drops of water trickled into her shoes. She reached the bottom of a hill only to find a rushing river blocking her way to where she knew their inn must be. She turned around and tried to climb up the hill again, but became exhausted and frightened. By this time, it was dark and the wind blew colder and harder. Margaret could see far below her a light that must have been the inn, but there was no way to get there. She was dressed for a summer day and her clothes were already wet and clammy. She described her plight in her journal:

[T]he prospect seemed appalling. I was very lightly clad,--my feet and dress were very wet,--I had only a little shawl to throw round me, and a cold autumn wind had already come, and the night-mist was to fall on me, all fevered and exhausted as I was. I thought I should not live through the night, or, if I did, live always a miserable invalid. There was no chance to keep myself warm by walking, for, now it was dark, it would be too dangerous to stir.

My only chance, however, lay in motion, and my only help in myself, and so convinced was I of this, that I did keep in motion the whole of that long night, imprisoned as I was on such a little perch of that great mountain. _How_ long it seemed under such circumstances only those can guess who may have been similarly circumstanced. The mental *experience of the time, most precious and profound,--for it was indeed a season lonely, dangerous, and helpless enough for the birth of thoughts beyond what the common sunlight will ever call to being,--may be told in another place and time.* (Fuller and Fuller 1860, 104)

Marcus Spring had never located the path by which they came up the mountain, but he finally found his way back to the inn and met a worried Rebecca and Eddie. They feared for Margaret's safety and sent shepherds out with their dogs to look for her. In the confusing mountain landscape, the shepherds could find no trace of her. They told the Springs, "No woman can live on the mountain tonight. The cold mists were coming when we came down."

To this Rebecca replied, "No common woman, but Margaret Fuller will not fold her hands and die." (Capper 2007, 286)

Morning finally came, bringing a heavy mist, so that Margaret could barely see the outline of the hill. At last she came to a spot where she could cross the river. The shepherds found her on the other side and took her back to the inn where the relieved Rebecca wrapped her in blankets and cared for her.

The long, frightening night had a strong effect on Margaret. While stranded on the cold dark mountainside, she had narrowly escaped death, and had spent solitary hours thinking about the end of her relationship with James Nathan and considering her future. The adventure was a transformative experience for her. In the days that followed, she turned with renewed vigor to her writing. Her brush with death somehow gave her greater self-confidence. She seemed to forget about Nathan and to move on to a new life with hope and courage.

After a few days rest, the party left the Highlands and traveled on to Glasgow. Here again Margaret was overwhelmed by the poverty and squalor, *"people are more crowded together and the stamp of squalid, stolid misery and degradation more obvious and appalling....I saw here in Glasgow persons, especially women, dressed in dirty, wretched tatters, worse than none, and with an expression of listless, unexpecting woe upon their faces..."* (Fuller, Reynolds and Smith 1991, 79)

Margaret and her friends then went south to England and eventually reached Newcastle, a city famous for its coalmines. With her usual curiosity, Margaret determined to visit a coalmine although most women would have been too afraid to try it. In her report for the *Tribune*, Margaret described it as "quite an odd sensation to be taken off one's feet and dropped down into darkness by the bucket." She felt sorry for the mine horses that spent their lives in the darkness hauling cars full of coal along the narrow tracks and never seeing daylight again once they had entered the mine. (Fuller, Reynolds and Smith 1991, 82)

In October, Margaret and the Springs finally arrived in London. Margaret was glad to have some quiet time to see the city: *"I am glad I did not at first see all that pomp and parade of wealth and luxury in contrast with the misery, squalid, agonizing, ruffianly, which stares one in the face in every street of London and hoots at the gates of her palaces....Poverty in England has terrors of which I never dreamed at home. I felt that it would be terrible to be poor there, but far more so to be the possessor of that for which so many thousands are perishing.*" (Fuller, Reynolds and Smith 1991, 88)

London was far larger than any American city. In 1841 the population was 1,948,417, and by 1851 when the next census was taken, five years after Margaret's visit, the city was home to 2,362,000 people. Poverty sent hundreds of poor people from every county in England and from famine-stricken Ireland to try their luck in London. There was no housing for these new inhabitants and by 1850, fifteen to twenty thousand homeless drifters or vagrants, many whole families, had to sleep in alleys or beneath the new railway arches. Dirt and disease were everywhere. Cholera epidemics, typhoid, tuberculosis, small pox and scarlet fever were constant threats. In 1849 alone, more than 50,000 people died in a cholera outbreak.

In spite of the poverty and dirt, London was a lively and vibrant city. Unlike the quiet streets of Boston, London was constantly noisy. In 1850, it was estimated that more than 5000 horses passed through the Temple Bar in one day with noisy hooves and noisome droppings. Omnibus drivers kept up a constant shout about their destinations. Peddlers cried out their wares at passers-by. The streets were filled with colorful figures—beggars, tradesmen, crowds of people trying to survive by any means they could devise.

Margaret was indignant about the poverty, which was far greater than any she had seen in America. She was pleased when she visited a public bathing and wash house. In her letter to the *Tribune* she described the establishment:

[T]he poor can go and hire, for almost nothing, good tubs, water ready heated, the use of an apparatus for rinsing,

drying and ironing, all so admirably arranged that a poor woman can in three hours get through an amount of washing and ironing that would, under ordinary circumstances, occupy three or four days. (Fuller, Reynolds and Smith 1991, 103)

Margaret remembered the hours of work she and her mother had spent washing, drying and ironing clothes for the family. She thought English housewives were wise to send out their laundry rather than trying to do it at home. She wrote that this custom should be adopted universally because washing day was so "malignant a foe to the peace and joy of households that it ought to be effaced from the calendar."

Margaret's reports from England were popular with readers of the *Tribune* because she described the details of everyday life that male reporters ignored. Circulation of the newspaper went up as more and more readers discovered her dispatches and enjoyed the lively language and anecdotes.

One of the things Margaret enjoyed most in England was meeting many famous people she had heard about. Many doors were open to her because her book *Women in the Nineteenth Century* was well-known and successful in London. At last she had a chance to meet her hero Thomas Carlyle whose writings she came to admire more and more as she traveled through England and saw the conditions about which he wrote.

Wherever there was fresh thought, generous hope, the thought of Carlyle has begun the work. He has torn off the veils from hideous facts; he has burnt away foolish illusions; he has awakened thousands to know what it is to be a man; that we must live, and not merely pretend to others that we live. (Fuller, Reynolds and Smith 1991, 100)

Despite her great admiration, she, like most people, found him difficult in social settings:

Accustomed to the infinite wit and exuberant richness of his writings, his talk is still an amazement and a splendor scarcely to be faced with steady eyes. He does not converse — only harangues…Carlyle allows no one a chance, but bears down all opposition, not only by his wit and onset of words resistless in their sharpness as so many bayonets, but actual physical superiority, raising his voice and rushing on his opponent with a torrent of sound. (Fuller, Reynolds and Smith 1991, 101)

Perhaps the man who made the greatest impression on her in the city was the Italian revolutionary leader, Giuseppe Mazzini. He was forty years old, only five years older than Margaret, and had been an active revolutionary in his native Italy for almost twenty years. He had founded Young Italy, a group dedicated to reuniting all of Italy under a democratic government. Because of his political activities, he had been imprisoned and finally banished to England. There he learned English so he could speak and write about the need for reform in Italy.

When they finally met, Margaret discovered that Mazzini was a handsome, charming man who always dressed in black, because, he explained, he was "in mourning for my country". She visited the school Mazzini had started in London for Italian boys. Most of them had been sold to unscrupulous businessmen by their parents, who were too poor to care for them. They were sent to England to work as organ grinders for almost no pay. Mazzini and his friends found these boys on the streets and taught them to read and write and to prepare for better jobs. Many Italian refugees in England donated their services to teach the boys.

Before leaving England, Margaret and the Springs apparently devised a plan to get a forged American passport for Mazzini so he could travel to Europe. Mazzini, however, had been sentenced to death in Italy and would be executed if he were caught, so he rejected the scheme. He did, however, appreciate Margaret's friendship and gave her letters of introduction to many of his friends in Paris. Meeting those people would soon change Margaret's life and bring her more excitement and danger than she had ever known.

Chapter 8: Encountering Paris (1846-1847)

After three months in England, Margaret and the Springs traveled to Paris, arriving on November 16. England had been a new experience for Margaret, but Paris was a whole new world. For the first time she would be in a country where people did not speak her language and where the customs and rules were very different. Unlike the "English cousins" who shared many literary interests and tastes with Americans, the French were exotic strangers. Furthermore, the intellectual classes of France lived with liberal ideas about sex and morals that were very different from those accepted in puritanical New England.

The Springs and Margaret stayed at the new Hotel Rougement on the Boulevard Poissonniere where Margaret wrote to her mother:

My room, though small, is very pretty, with the thick, flowered carpet and marble slabs, the French clock, with Cupid, of course, over the fireplace in which burns a bright little wood fire; the canopy bedstead, and inevitable large mirror; the curtains, too, are thick and rich, the closet, &cc., excellent, the attendance good. But for all this, one pays dear. We do not find that one can live pleasantly at Paris for little money; and we prefer to economize by a briefer stay if at all. (Fuller and Hudspeth 1983, 4:253)

Margaret's first step was to hire a French teacher to improve her French, so she would be prepared to meet the intellectuals she hoped to see. As she wrote to her brother Richard, "I have an excellent master every day, but to improve at the rate I ought to make use of my sojourn here I ought to learn even to think in French." (Fuller and Hudspeth 1983, 4:243) She was in a hurry to become fluent in French before using her letters of introduction to the actress, Rachel, and to the scandalous author George Sand. She was determined to meet George Sand even though many Americans would condemn her for visiting the author who was known as "the most licentious woman in Europe." (Deiss 1969, 41)

Like most tourists, Margaret was impressed by the beautiful fountains and monuments in Paris, but she must have been disturbed by the dirt of the streets. The population of Paris had reached one million, but it still had no centralized way to collect rubbish, which was tossed onto the streets. Only five thousand of the city's 224,000 households were connected with the ineffective sewer system. By comparison with Paris, London was a sweet-smelling city. Frances Trollope had visited the city ten years earlier and wrote scathing descriptions of the lack of sanitation:

It really appears to me that almost the only thing in the world which other men do, but which Frenchmen cannot, is the making of sewers and drains. After an hour or two of very violent rain last week, that part of the Place Louis-Quinze which is near the entrance to the Champs Elysees remained covered with water. The Board of Works having waited for a day or two to see what would happen, and finding that the muddy lake did not disappear, commanded the assistance of twenty-six able-bodied labourers, who set about digging just such a channel as little boys amuse themselves by making beside a pond. By this well-imagined engineering exploit, the stagnant water was at length conducted to the nearest gutter; the pickaxes were shouldered, and an open muddy channel left to adorn this magnificent area, which, were a little finishing bestowed upon it, would probably be the finest point that any city in the world could boast. (Trollope 1836, 116)

Not surprisingly, outbreaks of cholera swept through the city several times during the 1830s and 1840s; one in 1849, soon after Margaret's visit, caused 19,000 deaths. Margaret mentioned some of the French social problems in her dispatches to the *Tribune*, just as she had in England.

Margaret had a chance to experience Paris's modern medical treatment herself when a toothache started bothering her during her visit. She demonstrated her willingness to try new things by deciding to accept ether as a painkiller. As she wrote in a dispatch to the *Tribune*,

After suffering several days very much with the toothache, I resolved to get rid of the cause of sorrow by the aid of the Ether, not sorry, either, to try its efficacy, after all the marvelous stories I had heard. The first time I inhaled it, I did not for several seconds feel the effect.... [The dentist] then gave me the Ether in a stronger dose and this time I quitted the body instantly, and cannot remember any detail of what I saw and did...Again I started up, fancying that once more he had not dared to extract the tooth, but it was gone.... (Fuller, Reynolds and Smith 1991, 117)

Even though the lingering effects of the ether caused her some pain over the next few days, Margaret considered the experience was a great success.

Not all Parisians were as forward-looking as these doctors, as Margaret discovered when she went to the Sorbonne with Marcus Spring to hear a lecture by the well-known astronomer Urbain Jean LeVerrier. As she described it to her readers in the *Tribune*:

An old guardian of the inner temple seeing me approach had his speech all ready, and manning the entrance, said with a disdainful air, before we had time to utter a word. 'Monsieur may enter if he pleases, but Madame must remain here,' (i.e. in the court-yard). After some exclamations of surprise I found an alternative in the Hotel de Cluny where I passed an hour very delightfully while waiting for my companion. (Fuller, Reynolds and Smith 1991, 108)

Even after the lecture was over, Margaret was not allowed to see the hall in which it had been given, but was told by a guard that women were not permitted there: "What would you have, Madame, IT IS THE RULE" he insisted despite her pleas.

Margaret found some consolation in the theater, for which Paris was famous. "Here the theater is living; you see something really good, and good throughout" she told her readers. She looked forward to seeing the famous actress Rachel and was not disappointed. "I was sure that in her I should find a true genius, absolutely the diamond, and so it proved." Margaret attended each of the seven or eight performances Rachel gave during the Paris trip and reported that the actress had given her a new way of seeing French tragedy. "I had no idea of its powers and symmetry till now, and have received from the revelation high pleasure and a crowd of thoughts." (Fuller, Reynolds and Smith 1991, 104-5)

Unfortunately, Margaret was unable to meet Rachel who was so sought out that she often got a hundred letters a day and, according to her porter, usually threw them away unopened. (Capper 2007, 307) Margaret resigned herself to missing Rachel, but she searched for other artists, especially writers. She knew of Balzac and tried to find him but learned that he "frequented the lowest cafes….so that it was difficult to track him out" (Capper 2007, 313) Margaret was daring, but it was impossible for a woman to visit these places alone.

Finding George Sand was not easy either. Margaret had heard much in America about this woman who had deserted her husband and children to move to Paris with her lover and become a remarkably successful writer. When the love affair ended, she lived openly with several other lovers, although by the time Margaret arrived she had settled into a placid life with the Polish pianist Frederic Chopin. Even more shocking than her love life, perhaps, she sometimes dressed as a man so she could move around the city inconspicuously and go to places not open to women. Margaret was determined to discover the truth about her, because she believed the tales about her might have been exaggerated. But as she wrote to one friend "I find that all we have learned of her is true in the outline….She had every reason to leave her husband — a stupid, brutal man, who insulted and neglected her." (Fuller and Hudspeth 1983, 4:256) Despite having taken a series of lovers, Sand "takes her rank in society like a man, for the weight of her thoughts." Sand was not in Paris when Margaret arrived, but at her family home in Nohant, Berry. She did not respond to Margaret's first letter because she did not expect to return to Paris for another month.

When Margaret heard that Sand had returned to Paris on February 7, she took the initiative and called on her. After a somewhat awkward beginning, when Sand didn't realize who she was, the two got on very well. Margaret was impressed by Sand's "strong and masculine face" and her "lady-like dignity". (Capper

2007, 345) The two chatted for most of the afternoon and discovered they had much in common, especially a concern for the social problems of poverty and a desire to see more democracy and freedom in Europe. Despite her admiration and respect for Sand, however, Margaret did not write about her in letters to the *Tribune*. Americans were deeply prejudiced against French immorality, so perhaps Margaret, or Horace Greeley, decided a tribute to her would be too risky.

The individual who touched Margaret most deeply in Paris was the Polish patriot Adam Mickiewicz. He had been a famous poet and had written some of the best poetry of the nineteenth century, but had given up poetry to move to Paris and plot revolution. He was also a charismatic and extremely attractive man. Paris was home to many radical revolutionaries, although Mickiewicz's goal was more difficult than most. In order to free Poland and Lithuania (which he considered one country) both the czar of Russia and the emperor of Austria would have to be overthrown.

Mickiewicz had been the first professor of Slavic Literatures at the College de France but was forced to resign because of his attacks on the church. He was a deeply spiritual man who admired many of Margaret's transcendentalist friends and had quoted Emerson in his lectures. Margaret sent him a copy of Emerson's poems and invited him to come and see her, which he did. He dined with the Springs several times and often called on Margaret. His son Wladyslaw later recalled that "He made a strong impression upon her and in turn was astonished not so much at her masculine erudition as at the depth of her ideas and at the fact that they coincided with his own." (Capper 2007, 317) In their meetings they clearly felt some kind of spiritual bond and felt that they understood each other and shared common dreams. In a letter sent to her afterward, Mickiewicz wrote "Your spirit is linked with the history of Poland, of France and is beginning to link itself with the history of America." (Capper 2007, 318)

Margaret must have been moved by Mickiewicz lyric poetry if she found a translation from the Polish:

> O Sea! Within your unknown deeps concealed,
> When storms are wild, your monsters dream and sleep,
> And all their cruelty for the sunlight keep.
> Thus, Soul of Mine, in your sad deeps concealed
> The monsters sleep-when wild are storms. They Start
> From out some blue sky's peace to seize my heart.

(Mickiewicz 1917, 5)

Margaret later wrote to Emerson that Mickiewicz was the most important person she had met in Paris and she regretted the fact that this happened shortly before she left the city. "How much time had I wasted on others which I might have given to this real and important relation....it was only with Mickiewicz that I felt any deep-founded mental connection." (Fuller and Hudspeth 1983, 4:261)

With the inspiring talk of Mickiewicz still echoing in her mind, Margaret and the Springs left Paris on February 25, 1847 to make their way toward Italy—the country Margaret already called her spiritual home. As a child she had read the stories of ancient Romans and their bravery, as a young woman she had studied copies of Italian art, now at last she was to see the reality. Margaret and her friends planned to sail across the Mediterranean to Naples, but first made a side trip to Lyon and stopped to visit the weavers there. Margaret noted for her audience in the *Tribune* that the entire community, everyone from the age of nine, was engaged in the weaving trade. A young woman invited the party into her home where the large looms and some kitchen equipment took up most of the living area, while the family slept on beds kept on shelves near the ceiling which they reached by climbing a ladder.

Times were bad — the textile industry was one of the first casualties of the industrial revolution and factories were replacing the hand weavers, who struggled to get enough work to keep them going. They were often idle for weeks, and when they got a piece of work to do they kept at it until it was finished. Their employment was so irregular that children couldn't go to school because this would interfere with the family's weaving. As usual, Margaret was interested in the domestic arrangements of the women workers. The young woman who had befriended her boasted that she had nursed her two children herself rather than sending them out to a wet nurse as most working women did. Many children died from the poor care they received in these nurseries and Margaret noted that it would be a boon if the government would establish crèches which could be supervised and where children would receive adequate food and care. Prostitution was a great problem among the weavers because when work was slow, sending the women out to sell themselves was almost the only recourse a family had.

The contrast between the impoverished lives of the weavers in Lyon and the glamorous Parisians Margaret had seen earlier, was a sharp one. She and the Springs were now moving on to Italy, a country where poverty was greater than in France, and where wealth was even more ostentatious. From Lyon, she and the Springs went by carriage toward Avignon and then Marseilles for a ship to Italy, the country Margaret was most eager to see.

Chapter 9: Margaret Discovers Italy (1847)

The ship from Marseilles took the party to Genoa, the first Italian city Margaret had seen. She admired the lovely architecture of the city, but was especially impressed by the simple beauty and natural manners of the Italian people. As her friend the artist William Story noted, "All things are easy and careless in the out-of-doors life of the common people….One meets Nature at every turn—not braced up in prim forms, not conscious in manners, not made up into the fashionable or the proper; but impulsive, free and simple." (Deiss 1969, 48) From Genoa, Margaret and her friends traveled by coach to Rome because no railroad had been built in Italy. The government opposed industrial progress and did not welcome any of the innovations that were being developed in France and England. Even though the roads were in bad repair, Margaret was happy to travel on the ancient Via Appia, a road built by the Romans three hundred years before Christ's birth.

The Italy Margaret visited in 1847 was very different from the Roman Empire she had studied with her father. Ancient Rome had been the center of power in Europe, but the Italy of Margaret's time had very little power or influence. Unlike England or France, Italy was not a unified country but a collection of states each with its own government. Southern Italy, including Sicily, was the Kingdom of Naples ruled by King Ferdinand IV. The city of Rome and the surrounding area formed the Papal States ruled by the Pope, who was not only a religious but also a political leader. North of Rome lay the kingdom of Piedmont, the duchy of Tuscany, and the Austrian controlled areas of Lombardy and Venetia. Each of these small states was subject to interference from the large countries of France and Austria, which discouraged any attempt to introduce democratic governments.

Europe was in turmoil in 1847. The violence of the French Revolution, more than fifty years before, had shaken many members of ruling classes in every country and they had banded together to stabilize strong monarchies. Now the precarious peace brokered by the Austrian diplomat, Prince Metternich, at the Congress of Vienna in 1815 was unraveling. Driven by nationalism and liberalism, revolutionary parties appeared to threaten established monarchies in Austria, Russia, France and Italy. The severe economic conditions resulting from the beginnings of the Industrial Revolution caused discontent among farmers, peasants, and working people. Some of the exiled leaders Margaret had met in France were trying to bring democracy to Italy; so far, they had been unsuccessful. Margaret's visit came at a time when revolutionary forces were gathering strength. Mickiewicz's talk about the need for democracy and independence for Italy had impressed Margaret and she believed the revolutionaries might succeed in gaining power. In Rome, many people were hopeful that the new pope, Pius IX, would be willing to make changes to improve the lives of ordinary people. Margaret wrote approving of the pope, "He is a man of noble and good aspect who, it is easy to see, has set his heart on doing something good for the people."

Margaret and the Springs took rooms on the Via del Corso, a busy street where fashionable people walked, or rode in their carriages all day and late into the night. Margaret wrote to Emerson, "All night long, after the weather became fine, there was conversation or music before my window: I never really seemed to sleep while there." (Deiss 1969, 47) Adam Mickiewicz wrote to her from Paris that she should seek out Italians and learn to know them. Margaret started taking Italian lessons to improve her spoken Italian (she could already read the language) and set out to learn more about Rome.

Margaret continued to write her columns for the *Tribune.* Knowing her readers would be interested in Americans, Margaret visited the half dozen or so sculptors and painters who lived in the city. Some of them, like Christopher Cranch and William Story, she had known earlier in Boston. She also went to see the famous paintings of Michelangelo, Leonardo, Titian and other world famous painters of the Italian Renaissance. One of the Italian painters she learned most to appreciate during the trip was Titian. The beauty and power of his paintings, she felt, had not come through in the copies she had seen. She was disappointed to find that she was not always as impressed by the paintings as she had expected:

I cannot yet recover from my pain at finding the frescoes of Raphael in such a state enough to look at them happily. I had heard of it, but could not realize it. However, I have gained nothing by seeing his pictures in oil, which are well preserved. I find I had before the full impression of his genius. Michel Angelo's frescoes in like manner I seem to have seen as far as I can. But it is not the same with the sculptures:

my thought had not risen to the height of the Moses. It is the only thing in Europe, so far, which has entirely outgone my hopes. (Fuller, Reynolds and Smith 1991, 135)

Although she did not lose her interest in art, she could not keep her mind off the Italian political situation. She wrote to a friend, "Art is not important to me now...I take interest in the state of the people...I see the future dawning." (Deiss, p. 49) She spent time at the Caffe delle Belle Arti on the Corso which was a gathering place for people working for freedom and unity for all the Italian states. Talking of revolution was dangerous, but the secret police did not often interfere with the cafes where people gathered to drink coffee and smoke. At the cafes Margaret could hear news from all over the world and enjoy an excitement she had seldom felt in Boston.

On Easter Sunday, Margaret and the Springs went to vespers at St. Peter's church in Rome. Margaret stopped to look at one of the small altars, and became separated from the Springs. She wandered around the crowded church looking for them, confidant she would find them when the service was over. But when the service ended and people started leaving, she did not see them. As she stood waiting trying to decide what to do, a young Italian man approached her and asked if he could help her. He was handsome and dressed as a gentleman, so Margaret decided she could trust him. She explained what had happened and the two of them walked around the immense church hoping to find the Springs in some inconspicuous chapel. Eventually it became clear the Springs must have left the church and returned to their lodgings, probably thinking Margaret had joined one of the other parties of Americans at St. Peter's that day.

Margaret and the young man went outside to find a carriage but when it became clear none was available, her new friend offered to walk with Margaret back to her lodgings. As they walked, she learned more about him. His name was Giovanni Angelo Ossoli and he was several years younger than Margaret. His father, the Marchese Filippo Ossoli, was an officer at the papal court and his three older brothers were in service for the pope. The Ossoli were an old, noble family, which for generations had served the popes. Giovanni had chosen not to enter the papal service because, although he was a devout Catholic, he disapproved of the pope's political power.

During the weeks that followed, Margaret and Ossoli became close friends. Although Ossoli spoke no English, he understood French, so he and Margaret were able to carry on lively conversations in Italian and French. They shared the same views of politics and the importance of Italian unity. Ossoli was trained as a soldier, not a scholar, but he admired and appreciated Margaret's ideas and she valued his practical knowledge of Italy and Italians. She left no record of their courtship, but he visited Margaret often and took her to churches and other places of interest in the city.

The Ossoli family was a distinguished one in Rome. Their family chapel in the Church of the Maddalena, near the Pantheon displayed a seventeenth-century painting by Baciccia showing the Virgin and Saint Nicholas, the family's patron saint. Giovanni Ossoli's father was a younger son, and so not the head of the extended family, and he had three sons and two daughters of whom Giovanni was the youngest. The father was at this time in his seventies and very frail, so Giuseppe, the oldest son was in charge. More than twenty years older than Giovanni, and very conservative, Giuseppe was determined to uphold the family's reputation for support of the pope and the status quo. For years he had opposed Giovanni's sympathy with the Romans who wanted to increase secular power and secure more democracy for citizens. He would no doubt strongly oppose Giovanni's friendship with a Protestant American woman, much less condoned a marriage to her. When their father died in February 1848, the brothers' opposition became even more important because Giuseppe handled the father's estate. If Giovanni married against their wishes, he would probably never receive his share of his father's estate.

Margaret introduced Ossoli to the Springs, but their lack of Italian made conversation difficult. Marcus and Rebecca Spring thought Margaret's young friend was pleasant, and many years later Marcus Spring remembered that when they left Rome he had predicted Margaret would return and that she and Giovanni would eventually marry.

As the weeks went by, Margaret's relationship with Ossoli deepened, although she continued with her plans leave Rome with the Springs six weeks after Easter. Before she left, Ossoli proposed marriage. He was prepared to defy his family and marry Margaret despite their opposition. Margaret refused. "I loved him and felt very unhappy to leave him, but the connexion seemed so every way unfit. I did not hesitate a moment," she wrote to her sister Ellen. (Capper 2007,

332) Ossoli was ten years younger than she was and strongly attached to his family. She feared he would destroy his prospects for a future career if he married a foreigner disliked by his family. She told him she would leave Rome with the Springs but promised to return and see him again.

In June, Margaret and the Springs traveled to Florence. There they visited several American and English artists and writers who lived in the city. Sculptors Horatio Greenenough and Hiram Powers were working there and Margaret saw Greenenough's unfinished model of David as well as Powers' Greek Slave. They also met Italians, including the aristocratic Marchesa Costanza Arconati Visconti, who was active in the revolutionary movement. She and Margaret became good friends and would later work together in Rome.

Margaret enjoyed visiting the northern Italian cities and wrote about them for her *Tribune* readers, but she kept thinking about Giovanni Ossoli. The Springs wanted to continue their travels by going to Switzerland and Germany as planned, but Margaret longed to stay in Italy. Finally, they decided to separate. In October, Margaret returned to Rome and took an apartment in the home of an Italian noblewoman. An inheritance of four hundred dollars from her Uncle Abraham had given Margaret enough money to plan on living in Italy for six months.

While continuing to write her letters to the *Tribune*, Margaret took on a larger project. She decided to write a history of modern Italy. She wanted Americans to learn more about what the country was going through and how it was struggling to become a democratic state. She gathered together books and papers about the current situation and began to study them. At the same time, she continued her social life, seeing many of the Americans living in Rome, but spending most of her time with Ossoli. Through him, she was introduced to many young Italians.

Margaret tried to attend all of the meetings of political groups to sample different opinions about how to solve Rome's problems. The streets were filled with beggars who had no chance of finding work. The conservative papal government did not try to stimulate business of any kind. Most people were illiterate and education was discouraged except for a tiny elite. While the rest of Europe was developing trade and becoming prosperous, Italy remained poor and backward. Revolutionary hopes were high! As an American, Margaret felt she had a responsibility to understand the history and respect the traditions of Italy. At the same time, she wanted to demonstrate to Italians the benefits of American democracy and enterprise. "The American in Europe," she wrote to her *Tribune* readers, "if a thinking mind, can only become more American." (Fuller, Reynolds and Smith 1991, 161) She knew Italians were struggling with some of the same issues Americans had argued about before their revolution. Now that the United States was thriving, Margaret hoped Americans would not turn their backs on other countries trying to free themselves from the tyranny of absolute monarchies and privileged nobles.

While Margaret was busy with the serious work of writing, she had time to enjoy a happy private life. In December of 1847, she wrote to her mother, "My life at Rome is thus far all I hoped. I have not been so well since I was a child, nor so happy ever as during the last six weeks." (Fuller and Hudspeth 1983, 4:312) Although she did not tell her mother or her friends about Giovanni, it was undoubtedly being with him that made her so happy. For the first time in her life, Margaret had found a man who admired and loved her for what she was. Despite the differences in their backgrounds, their love was growing.

Chapter 10: Rome Prepares for Battle (1847-1848)

When Margaret returned to Rome in October 1847, she found the city stirring with new energy. Although she must have been preoccupied with her relationship with Ossoli, she did not lose interest in political events. The two of them grew closer because of their shared hope for revolutionary changes. Much of Europe was in turmoil during the explosive years of 1847-1848, and Italy, divided into numerous small states and nations, was ripe for change.

Because the Roman government was controlled by religious leaders, many people believed it would be sinful to question its authority; nonetheless, the pope was under pressure to allow the citizens of Rome some voice in the running the government. In the summer of 1847 he had established a Council of State, whose members would include not only priests but also other leading citizens. This Council marked the first time lay people were allowed a voice in the government. This council would deal with practical problems such as providing gaslights on the streets and encouraging industry.

When the Council was inaugurated in September, there was great rejoicing at this step toward a more democratic state. Romans planned street demonstrations. Margaret reported to her readers in the *Tribune* that the small colony of Americans in Rome decided they should show support by flying the

American flag. They soon discovered there was not an American flag available in Rome and Margaret describes the flurry that followed:

> *So they hurried to buy their silk — red, white and blue, and inquired of recent arrivals how many States there are this Winter in the Union, in order to making [sic] the proper number of stars. A magnificent spread Eagle was procured, not without difficulty…. This eagle having previously spread its wings over a piece of furniture where its back was sustained by the wall was somewhat deficient in a part of its anatomy. But we flattered ourselves he should be held so high that no Roman eye, if disposed, could carp and criticize. When lo! Just as the banner was ready to unfold its young glories in the home of Horace, Virgil and Tacitus, an ordinance appeared, prohibiting the display of any but the Roman ensign.* (Fuller, Reynolds and Smith 1992, 174-175)

As Margaret became more caught up in Italian life, her relationship with Ossoli and discussions about politics, she was increasingly critical of some of the other Americans who visited Italy without trying to understand the country. She wrote to one correspondent, "Since I have experienced the different atmosphere of the European mind, nay, mingled in the bonds of love, I suffer more than ever from that which is peculiarly American or English. I should like to cease hearing the language for a time." (Deiss 1969, 92)

In her letters to the *Tribune*, Margaret urged her fellow citizens to take a greater interest in European affairs. She congratulated the American sculptors Horatio Greenough and Thomas Crawford who had publicly supported the Republican cause. She was highly critical, however, of many other Americans in Rome, writing:

I am sorry to say that a large portion of my countrymen here take the same slothful and prejudiced view as the English, and, after many years' sojourn, betray entire ignorance of Italian literature and Italian life....they talk about the corrupt and degenerate state of Italy as they do about that of our slaves at home. They come ready trained to that mode of reasoning which affirms that, because men are degraded by bad institutions, they are not fit for better.
(Deiss 1969, 92-93)

Despite her disappointment in the political scene, and her disillusionment with some of her countrymen, Margaret was very happy in Rome. At some point during that winter Ossoli and Margaret became lovers. Despite her rigid Protestant upbringing, Margaret believed love should be expressed fully whether or not marriage was an option. Marriage to a non-Catholic would have required Ossoli to obtain a papal dispensation, and for that he would have to let his family know of the marriage, which would give his eldest brother a reason to cut him off from any inheritance. Margaret was not willing to ask that of him. She had a strong appreciation of the value of money and the importance of having funds to support a marriage and family.

The final weeks of 1847 were dark and rainy in Rome. The streets were rivers of mud making it difficult for horses to pull carriages and almost impossible for a woman to navigate in long skirts and flimsy shoes. But Margaret had more than the weather to worry about. She was pregnant with Ossoli's child.

While Margaret worried about her personal dilemma, 1848 ushered in an exciting new year for Europe. The conservative Alexis de Tocqueville rose in the Chamber of Deputies in Paris to warn his colleagues that sooner or later the discontent would explode. "I believe that right now we are sleeping on a volcano….can you not sense that the earth is trembling again in Europe? Can you not feel…the wind of revolution in the air?" (Rapport 2008, 42) The first dramatic events came not in France, but in Italy.

Young nobles in Milan were frustrated in their attempts to advance themselves in the German-speaking government of the Austrian empire that ruled the region. They decided to hit the Austrians in their most vulnerable place—the treasury. Inspired by the Boston Tea Party, they organized a boycott of tobacco, because the tobacco tax was a significant source of revenue. Lower class people joined in, because they resented having to pay taxes to Austria. On New Year's Day 1848 the Milanese gave up smoking; Austrians retaliated by increasing their smoking, often waving cigars in the faces of the young Italians. After a few days, the inevitable violence started when an Italian knocked a cigar out of an Austrian's mouth precipitating a fight that soldiers quickly broke up. In doing so, they beat up some Italian citizens and a larger crowd gathered and attacked the troops, thus starting a "tobacco riot" which resulted in the death of six civilians and the wounding of fifty. News of the uprising soon spread throughout Italy.

Margaret was afraid that the Pope's new Council of State was not a sign that he really welcomed change, but only that he was reacting to the spirit of the times. She was proved right when, as the struggle of Milan against Austrian rule became more intense, he pulled back on reforms. He was unwilling to fight against another Catholic state, fearing a weakening of the Church. Pressure from the revolutionary leaders increased as the Pope tried to slow down reform and called for a day of prayer for peace. This brought on a night-time demonstration on February 3, in which torch-bearing marchers filled the Corsi. The Romans still cheered for the Pope, but now they also cheered the new Civic Guard. During the next few days rumors spread that the Austrians would send troops to restore order, and another demonstration filled the Plaza del Popolo. Demonstrators called on the Pope to raise an army to defend the frontiers.

Margaret struggled to keep up with the ever-changing political activities in Italy, but the first three months of 1848 were very difficult for her. In March, she wrote for her *Tribune* readers: "It is long since I have written; my health entirely gave way beneath the Roman Winter. The rain was constant, commonly falling in torrents from the 17th December to the 19th March. Nothing could surpass the dirt, the gloom, the desolation of Rome." (Fuller, Reynolds and Smith 1991, 209) The weather was not all that was oppressing her. She had severe morning sickness from her secret pregnancy and suffered almost constantly from nausea and headaches.

By April, Margaret realized she would have to leave the city if she hoped to conceal her pregnancy. As the months went by, even the long skirts and bulky dresses of the day would not hide her condition. She and Ossoli decided she should move to a small town outside of Rome, close enough for him to visit frequently but far enough away, so her friends would not try to visit her. They told no one where she was living. Her mail was sent to her banker in Rome, where Ossoli picked it up and brought it to her.

Margaret took rooms in the town of Aquila in the mountains of Abruzzi about fifty miles east of Rome. In a letter to a friend, Margaret described the environment as being very beautiful "I am in the midst of a theatre of mountains, some of them crowned with snow, all of very noble shapes.....through the valley glides a little stream, along its banks here and there little farm houses..." (Fuller and Hudspeth 1983, 5:77) In the midst of this beauty, however, Margaret was isolated from everyone she knew. Ossoli could not leave his position with the Civil Guard in Rome except for short Sunday visits. (Deiss 1969, 146) Meanwhile Emerson was in London and wrote often urging her to return to America with him. He wrote that her friends and family missed her and could not understand why she stayed away so long. Margaret could not explain. She knew Emerson would be shocked if she appeared in London so obviously pregnant.

Alone in the mountains, Margaret tried to work on her history of Italy, but found it difficult to concentrate. She was preoccupied with plans for the future. And writing an account of the revolution in Rome was a massive undertaking. Her readers in America knew very little about the Italian situation and she struggled to explain the constantly changing politics.

Encouraged by the changes in Sicily and fighting in Milan, Italian revolutionaries who had fled into exile years earlier returned. Giuseppe Mazzini, who had lived in London for eighteen years, was finally able to see Italy again. Giuseppe Garibaldi, who had been exiled after an unsuccessful 1834 rebellion, returned from South

America where he had lived for twelve years. Every week brought changes as one Italian ruler after another gave citizens a constitution with a promise of greater democracy.

After two months of isolation in Aquila, Margaret decided to move to Rieti, a small town closer to Rome. Although the risk of discovery was slightly greater, she wanted to be closer to Ossoli so he could visit more often. She was not writing any letters for the *Tribune* that summer because of a misunderstanding about money with Horace Greeley. Margaret had asked him for an advance. Although he was hard pressed himself, he sent the money to her old banker in London. Through some mix up it was sent to Paris and not forwarded to Rome as it should have been. Margaret worried about money and Horace Greeley wondered why she did not send any columns to the newspaper.

August was a discouraging month. Margaret would have loved to be in Rome where the revolutionary party was struggling to bring greater democracy. Instead she had to remain in Rieti awaiting the birth of her child, alone, unhappy, and unwell. She was afraid she might die in childbirth; at the age of thirty-eight giving birth was often dangerous. She sent small gifts to family members with notes asking them not to forget her. Ossoli's visits cheered her, but he could spend very little time with her.

Finally, on September 5, 1848, her waiting was over. Her son, Angelo Eugenio Fillipo Ossoli, was born. It was a difficult birth and Margaret was attended by a midwife and a village doctor. Ossoli was with Margaret when the baby was born, but had to return to Rome the next morning. Angelino, as his parents called him, was a healthy child, and Margaret herself recovered from the childbirth successfully.

She struggled with the unfamiliar task of caring for a baby who often cried and fussed, but she had two Italian women to help her. Every day she wrote letters to Ossoli full of news of young Angelino, who grew bigger and stronger every day. She worried about his health, especially when smallpox broke out in Rieti and the supply of vaccine was used up. A firm believer in modern medical practices, Margaret was determined to get vaccine for her baby. After several anxious letters back and forth, Ossoli was able to send vaccine from Rome and Margaret found a doctor to vaccinate the baby.

As the weeks went by, she worried about whether she should take Angelino to Rome when she returned or leave him in the safety of Rieti. She wrote to Ossoli suggesting they try to find a nurse in Rome, but he wanted the baby to stay in Rieti so their secret would not be discovered. Finally, by the beginning of November, she found a nurse in Rieti with whom she was willing to leave the baby. Before leaving, she arranged to have the baby baptized so his birth would be recorded properly.

Although she missed her child, Margaret was happy to return to Rome. "You cannot conceive the enchantment of this place," she wrote to her mother. "Those have not lived who have not seen Rome." (Fuller and Hudspeth 1983, 5:147) She went on to tell her mother the exciting news in the city. In late September, Pope Pius IX had appointed Pellegrino Rossi, the former ambassador from France, to be his chief minister, but many Italians resented having a French citizen named as the pope's right hand man. Rossi attracted further criticism when he tried to cool revolutionary fervor by clamping down on press freedom. On November 15, as Rossi got out of his carriage to enter the Chamber of Deputies, the crowd hissed and pushed him. When he turned to see who had attacked him, he was stabbed to death. The soldiers standing by at the Chambers watched silently and did nothing as the assassin disappeared in the crowd. "I never thought to hear of a violent death with satisfaction," Margaret wrote, "but this act affected me as one of terrible justice". (Fuller and Hudspeth 1983, 5:147)

The next day hundreds of people and many troops marched to the Pope's residence to demand a change in government. The Swiss Guards were called out to protect the Pope. Although the Pope agreed to see a representative of the group, he rejected all demands for change. When a mob of people tried to enter the palace, the Pope's personal force, the Swiss guards, opened fire on them.

The turmoil continued for several days. Parliament was unable to function, because people in the gallery screamed down any conservative or even moderate speakers. The Pope's friends and supporters were afraid to visit him except in secret. Finally the Pope could take it no longer. On the evening of November 24, he put on the plain cassock of an ordinary priest and slipped into a carriage and out of the papal palace. He fled to the Kingdom of Naples, where he took refuge in the coastal city of Gaeta. Margaret and Ossoli celebrated along with many other Romans. The way was now clear for a new republican government. The future seemed full of hope for them and their son.

Chapter 11: Republican Rome (1849)

In December 1848, the misunderstanding with Horace Greeley about payments sent to Paris was finally cleared up and Margaret began writing columns for the *Tribune* again. Now she could stop worrying quite so much about expenses, because Greeley's payments for the columns would pay for the nurse in Rieti who was caring for Angelino and for anything the baby needed. Now that her son had survived the first few months of his life, always the most dangerous time for a child, Margaret was prepared to tell a few friends about him. She wrote to her best friend, Caroline Sturgis Tappan, who also had a new baby. Although she knew it was difficult to keep a secret, she asked Caroline to tell no one about her baby. Margaret hoped she would be able to share the news with her family and friends in her own way when she was ready, but she didn't want her mother and sisters to worry about her now.

Now at last Margaret could return to Rome and see for herself what was happening. Many foreigners had fled the city, so rents were lower and she was able to find an inexpensive apartment in the upper story of a house on the Piazza Barberine. She had only one room, but, as she wrote to her mother, it was "large; and everything about the bed so gracefully and adroitly disposed that it makes a beautiful parlor....I have the sun all day, and an excellent chimney. It is very high and has pure air and the most beautiful view all around imaginable." (Deiss 1969, 182) Her landlords were a delightful old couple, and fellow residents in the house included a friendly elderly priest, an English woman and a Russian princess.

Margaret, Ossoli, and their Italian friends had high hopes for a more democratic Rome under the new Republican government, but life was uncertain. Banks were reluctant to accept the new money being printed by the revolutionary government. When Margaret finally received money from America, she had great difficulty converting it into Roman money for her expenses. Everyday problems tormented her and she constantly had to worry about money. She begged her American friends to write letters on very thin paper so she would not have to pay excessive postage charges. Cash was short and postage had to be paid by the person receiving the letter, not the one who sent it. Even when her family tried to pay the postage ahead, there was no arrangement with the Roman government to allow this. Much of her mail was lost and she worried about what was going on at home.

In her dispatches to the *Tribune*, Margaret tried to describe to Americans the exciting revolution that was occurring in Rome and across Italy. The winter of 1848-49, unlike the cold rainy winter the year before, was one of the warmest and driest in years. When Carnival time came in February, Margaret wrote:

The Republican Carnival has not been as splendid as the Papal; the absence of Dukes and Princes being felt in the way of coaches and rich dresses, are also fewer than usual; many having feared to assist at this most peaceful of revolutions. But, if less splendid, it was not less gay; the costumes were many and the fanciful – flowers, smiles and fun abundant. ****Many handsome women, otherwise dressed in white, wore the red liberty cap, and the noble though

somewhat coarse Roman outline beneath this brilliant red, by
the changeful glow of million lights, made a fine effect.
(Fuller, Reynolds and Smith 1991, 247-8)

The red liberty caps, borrowed from those worn during the French Revolution, were a symbol of liberty across Europe. The Romans, and Margaret herself, hoped democracy would spread across the continent. She knew it might take a long time but predicted: "All Europe...is to be under republican government in the next century." (Deiss 1969, 220)

Americans could help the nations of Europe, especially Italy, in the struggle primarily by sending a good Ambassador, by which Margaret meant a man who had experience of foreign life, good judgment, and the ability to look beyond party politics in the United States. She even added: "Another century, and I might ask to be made Ambassador myself ('tis true, like other Ambassadors, I would employ clerks to do the most of the duty,) but woman's day had not come yet." (Fuller, Reynolds and Smith 1991, 245)

Americans in general knew very little about what was going on in Italy, and many were not sympathetic to the revolutionary movements, even though they echoed the actions of Americans only a few generations earlier. Italians were considered too volatile and primitive to handle a democratic revolution and establish a Republic.

Many thoughtful people were impressed by Margaret's first-hand accounts of what was going on in Rome, because they countered the wild rumors about vicious anti-clerical radicals attacking priests and churches, which were circulated in both British and American papers. Margaret was the only reporter based in Rome and her letters to the *Tribune* were widely circulated and respected. Even the conservative Southern Literary Messenger wrote of her dispatches, "No one can call in question the intellectual vigor they display, whatever antagonism of opinion they may excite." (Capper 2007, 424) Ever since the Parisian workers uprising in Paris the previous spring, many Americans were becoming increasingly skeptical about European revolutions.

While Americans discussed whether the Italian revolution was worthy of support, the Republican government itself was fighting to maintain its control of the city. Ever since the pope had fled the city, European leaders had been determined to have him regain his power. Both Catholic and non-Catholic governments were worried about the spread of revolution and republicanism. Most Italians thought the principal threat was from the Austrians in the North, but when trouble came it was from France. Margaret had warned about danger from France and its newly elected president Louis-Napoleon Bonaparte, nephew of the former emperor. She wrote in her journal in March, after hearing that the French government had refused to receive the Roman ambassador, "The French government will not be friendly to the Italian republics." (Capper 2007, 427)

On April 24, French forces landed at Civita Vecchia, the port closest to Rome. The French leader, General Oudinot, announced that the army came as a friend to the Romans. Nonetheless, when General Oudinot's aide arrived in Rome, he declared that the French were determined to restore the Pope to power. Mazzini took this message to the assembly, which voted unanimously not to allow the French forces into the city.

Instead they vowed to save the Republic and to repulse force with force. (Deiss 1969, 231)

On April 27, Garibaldi led his troops into Rome while the people cheered his entry. The Civic Guard in which Ossoli was serving was ready to fight. And Margaret took up her duties at the Hospital of the Fate Bene Fratelli. She was soon to see far more of war than she had ever dreamed.

The French troops marching toward Rome had been told they would be welcomed by the people. Instead, they found the roads almost deserted except for a few hostile, sullen peasants. The French had little to fear in fighting. They were a well-trained and disciplined army of six thousand men. Rome was defended by about three thousand volunteers, about three hundred of them students, and one thousand of them members of the national guard (including Ossoli) who had never seen action in a battle or faced enemy soldiers. These volunteers were strengthened by twenty five hundred papal troops who had gone over to the Republican side taking their weapons with them. Although the numbers were fairly equal, the French soldiers fought as a unit while the Romans were disorganized and without experienced leaders.

During the siege, Margaret had little time to write. She was caught up in the action. Her friend William Story described Rome on the eve of the French attack:

April 30 Expectation of the hourly approach of the French. All the streets deserted, gloomy and morose, as before some terrible thunderstorm. The women were all fled to the houses, save here and there one whom curiosity had led out. The shops all shut, with here and there a door half open and revealing the form of a soldier peering out....at about one *o'clock we heard the pealing cannon and knew the battle had* *begun.* (Deiss 1969, 236)

A few days later, on May 6th, 1849, Margaret wrote to the *Tribune* "I write to you from barricaded Rome. The Mother of Nations is now at bay against them all." (Fuller, Reynolds and Smith 1991, 274) Margaret realized Rome could not stand against all the forces combined against it. She admired the bravery of the Italians who fought to preserve their Republic despite the bombardment. The French troops were camped a few miles outside of Rome awaiting further orders from Paris. One of Margaret's concerns was the destruction of the beautiful art of Rome. On May 27, she wrote:

War near at hand seems to me even more dreadful than *I had fancied it. ...Here, it has produced much fruit of noble* *sentiment, noble act; but still it breeds vice, too, drunkenness,* *mental dissipation, tears asunder the tenderest ties, lavishes* *the productions of earth for which her starving poor stretch* *out their hands in vain, in the most unprofitable* *manner....Rome is shorn of the locks which lent grace to her* *venerable brow. She looks desolate, profaned.* (Fuller, Reynolds and Smith 1991, 280)

The fighting went on through May and June. Margaret continued her work in the hospital. Although she had longed for the revolution and cheered on the troops, she was horrified by the pain and suffering all around her. In June she wrote

Since April 30, I go daily to the hospitals, and though I *have suffered for I had no idea how terrible gunshot wounds* *and wound fever are — yet I have taken pleasure, and great*

pleasure, in being with the many. There is scarcely one who is not moved by a noble spirit. (Marraro 1932, 77)

The house where Margaret lived became filled with people fleeing from heavily-hit areas of the city. On July 6, Margaret wrote:

After the 22nd, the slaughter of the Romans became every day more fearful. Their defenses were knocked down by the heavy cannon of the French, and, entirely exposed...great numbers perished on the spot. Those who were brought into the Hospitals were generally grievously wounded, very commonly subjects for amputation. My heart bled daily more and more at these sights, and I could not feel much for myself, though now the balls and bombs began to fall round me also. (Fuller, Reynolds and Smith 1991, 303)

On July 4, a day that Americans celebrate their independence, the Romans lost theirs. The French army entered the city and General Oudinot declared the papal government restored in Rome. Garibaldi led his forces out of the city determined to carry on the fight. After severe hardships and the loss of many of his men, he managed to reach Venice. Mazzini, with Margaret's help in getting a passport, managed to get to Switzerland and eventually to London. It would be another twenty years before these men saw Italy finally united and free of foreign domination.

Margaret's letter to the *Tribune* after the fall of the Republic was a plea for Americans to help other countries gain the freedom that they enjoyed. "Send money, send cheer, acknowledge as the legitimate leaders and rulers those men who represent the people....Friends, countrymen, and lovers of virtue, lovers of freedom, lovers of truth! Be on the alert; rest not supine in your easier lives, but remember: 'Mankind is one, and beats with one great heart'." (Fuller, Reynolds and Smith 1991, 311; quotation from Bailey's "Festus")

In her private letters, Margaret sounded even more dispirited and discouraged. On July 9, 1849, she wrote to her brother Richard:

I received two or three weeks ago your letter of the 4th May. Probably I shall answer it, sometime, if I should ever again find myself tranquil and recruited from the painful excitements of these last sad days. But amid the ruined hopes of Rome, the shameful oppressions she is beginning to suffer, amid these noble bleeding martyrs, my brothers, I cannot fix my thoughts on anything else..... (Fuller and Hudspeth 1983, 5:243-244)

While waiting for the pope to return, the city was run by a group of three cardinals who reinstated many of the old papal rules including strict censorship of newspapers. The French were really in charge, however, and they wanted to ensure the city would remain peaceful while waiting for the pope's return. They imposed the death sentence on anyone who harassed a French soldier. Margaret recorded that "Three families were carried to prison because a boy crowed like a cock at the French soldiers." (Deiss 1969, 275) Even more appalling to Margaret, the French told the wounded men in hospitals they would have to leave in eight days; those who were too weak to leave their beds would be transferred to the Termini prison.

Margaret's thoughts were on her own little boy who had remained in Rieti during the siege in Rome. As she wrote later to Caroline Sturgis "During all the siege of Rome I could not see him, and...I often seemed to hear him calling me amid the roar of the cannon, and he seemed to be crying." (Fuller and Hudspeth 1983, 5:238) Her fears were raised even higher when she received a letter from Horace Greeley opening with the sentence, "Ah, Margaret, the world grows dark with us! You grieve for Rome is fallen;--I mourn, for Pickie is dead." (Fuller and Hudspeth 1983, 5:259) Pickie had been a toddler when Margaret lived with the Greeleys and she had spent many afternoons playing with him. He was the Greeleys' only son and he had been struck down by a sudden summer fever.

With the Roman Republic defeated, Ossoli was in great danger. He had lived his entire life in Rome and had many ties there, but even his family would not defend him now. He and Margaret had to decide where they would be safe to live and raise their son. Margaret knew they would have to leave Rome, but she was anguished. She wrote to her friend William Channing:

I cannot tell you what I endured in leaving Rome; abandoning the wounded soldiers; knowing that there is no provision made for them, when they rise from the beds where they have been thrown by a noble courage, where they have suffered with a noble patience. Some of the poorer men, who rise bereft even of the right arm, – one having lost both the right arm and the right leg, – I could have provided for with a small sum. Could I have sold my hair, or blood from my arm, I would have done it. (Fuller, Channing, and Emerson 1857)

Despite the pain of leaving, Margaret knew she had to take care of her family. Her husband's safety depended on leaving the city. Resolutely she gathered together a few of their belongings and on July 12, she and Ossoli left Rome and headed for Rieti.

Chapter 12: Refuge in Florence

When Margaret and Ossoli arrived in Rieti they found their fears about Angelino were justified. During the siege, communications between Rome and Rieti had been cut and when the family that boarded Angelino didn't hear from Margaret, they feared the baby had been abandoned. The wet nurse took on the care of another child and Angelino did not get enough nourishment. Margaret and Ossoli were shocked when they saw him; as she wrote in her Fuller, Channing, and Emerson 1857, "*And when I came, I found mine own fast waning to the tomb! His nurse, lovely and innocent as she appeared, had betrayed him, for lack of a few scudi! He was worn to a skeleton; his sweet, childish grace all gone! Everything I had endured seemed light to what I felt when I saw him too weak to smile, or lift his wasted little hand. Now, by incessant care, we have brought him back, – who knows if that be a deed of love? – into this hard world once more. But I could not let him go, unless I went with him; and I do hope that the cruel law of my life will, at least, not oblige us to be separated. . When I saw his first returning smile, – that poor, wan, feeble smile! – and more than four weeks we watched him night and day, before we saw it, – new resolution dawned in my heart. I resolved to live, day by day, hour by hour, for his dear sake.* This second blow to her hopes left Margaret feeling deep despair, "I am tired of thinking, tired of hoping," she wrote to a friend (Deiss 1969, 279). Still, she rallied to make plans for taking her husband and baby to safety in Florence.

While they were in Rieti, Ossoli made a last attempt to retrieve some of the family money that was due him. He set off to visit his brothers to talk about selling some of the small properties he had inherited. When he did not return by nightfall, Margaret panicked, and was not any happier when she heard in the morning he had been detained by the police for straying into the territories of the Kingdom of Naples. The problem seemed to be that he was traveling with an American passport given to him by Lewis Cass, the American ambassador in Rome. Although this was perfectly legal because he was married to an American, Margaret worried that it would lead to a long delay. As it happened, the soldiers holding Ossoli noticed a letter addressed to Marchese Ossoli in his pocket, realized he had a title, and set him free. He did not manage, however, to obtain any of the money due him. His brothers would no longer speak to him at all; and, although his sister tried to help him and Margaret, she could not influence any family financial decisions.

Giving up hope of obtaining any money in Rome, Margaret and Ossoli started out for Florence. At least there they would be safe from harassment by the pope and his supporters. The distance between Rieti and Florence is just under 200 miles through hilly countryside much of it covered with vineyards. That was a long journey in the mid-nineteenth century, especially when traveling with a young baby. They broke their trip in Perugia and stayed for several days.

The journey gave them a peaceful break after the weeks of strain and suffering. In Perugia they visited local churches and Margaret had time to read and rest, while Angelino gained strength every day. Soon they continued on their way to Florence: "*Our journey here was delightful,*" Margaret wrote in her journal, "*it is the first time I have seen Tuscany when the purple grape hangs garlanded from tree to tree. We were in the early days of the vintage: the fields were animated by men and women, some of the latter with such pretty little bare feet, and shy, soft eyes, under the round straw hat. They were beginning to cut the vines, but had not done enough to spoil any of the beauty."* (Fuller, Channing, and Emerson 1857) Their first glimpse of Florence as the carriage rolled across the hills must have been striking. They traveled beside the green waters of the Arno River between its deep banks and coming over a hill finally saw the great dome of the cathedral in the distance and beyond it the peaks of the Apennines.

Margaret's arrival in Florence created a sensation among the American and British colony there. Elizabeth Barrett Browning wrote that Margaret had:

...taken us by surprise at Florence, retiring from the Roman world with a husband and child above a year old. Nobody had even suspected a word of this underplot, and her American friends stood in mute astonishment... (Deiss 1969, 288)

The news that Margaret had a baby and a husband spread quickly among the Americans in the city. Margaret knew people were talking about her, but she did not feel the interest as unfriendly. She wrote to her old friend Costanza Visconti:

I have been a little surprised at the even increased warmth of interest with which the little American society of Florence has received me, with the unexpected accessories of husband and child, asking no questions and seemingly content to find me so. With you I indeed thought it would be so, because you are above the world; (Fuller and Hudspeth 1983, 5:269)

Margaret was optimistic in her assessment of the situation. People talked about her new husband and baby and wondered why she had not told anyone about the situation earlier. Gossip was spreading in America after the news arrived there. Margaret had written to her mother just before she left Rome, telling her about Ossoli and Angelino. She described Ossoli to her mother and wrote "I am sure that you will love him very much, and that he will love you no less." (Fuller and Hudspeth 1983, 5:261)

Margaret's family and friends had mixed reactions to news of the marriage. Fortunately, for Margaret, her mother and sister were happy to hear about Ossoli and the baby Angelino. Despite the conventional background of Margaret's mother, she was willing to brave the criticism of her neighbors and support Margaret. She knew some people would question whether a marriage had ever taken place and whether the baby might be illegitimate. The stigma of having a daughter with an illegitimate baby was a major source of embarrassment to New England families at that time. It was not unlikely that some people would stop talking to the Fullers and would no longer invite them to tea parties or other events. Many mothers would have refused to accept Ossoli as a son-in-law, but Margaret's mother had strong faith in Margaret's account of what had happened. Margaret's sister, Ellen, who had married the charming, but irresponsible poet Ellery Channing and was suffering through her own tumultuous marriage, had only good wishes for Margaret. They understood her decision not to tell them sooner and wrote that they looked forward to seeing the family when they returned to America. Margaret's brothers were less willing to accept her unconventional behavior. Her brother Richard refused to write to her and Arthur was disturbed that a scandal might affect the whole family. They were afraid people would find it odd that Margaret had married a man who spoke very little English and was not particularly interested in literature or social issues. It was not considered a suitable marriage for one of the leading New England intellectuals.

Margaret found the cosmopolitan American and British colony in Florence more accepting of her new status than the people back home. Most of the Americans in the city were artists. The sculptor Horatio Greenough and his wife, who had lived abroad for several years, became good friends. Greenough liked Ossoli and accepted him easily. In a letter to his brother, he wrote "Marquis Ossoli (about whom there has been a great deal of misapprehension) was singularly grave and dignified,--the only Italian we ever met who had not the national vivacity and expressive gesture....appearing self-poised and truthful" (Greenough 1887, 217) Horace Sumner, son of Timothy Fuller's old friend Charles Sumner, had been an admirer of Margaret every since he had seen her at Brook Farm. He came every day to call, bringing flowers and offering to exchange English lessons for Italian lessons from Ossoli.

Margaret was finally enjoying a normal family life with her husband and child; Ossoli too enjoyed Florence and did not regret his loss of the familiar sights and sounds of Rome. However, they still had concerns about money. Despite Margaret's fame, she did not receive much money for her writing; she continued to write letters for the *Tribune* for a while from Florence, but Horace Greeley seemed less enthusiastic about her work. He probably worried because the gossip in New York about Margaret's marriage and her radicalism threatened the paper's circulation. Margaret's major hope for earning money was to finish her history of the Roman revolution and find a publisher. Although she was happy to see old friends, Margaret avoided getting too caught up in the social life of the American colony and worked on her book every afternoon while Angelino napped.

The decision that faced Margaret was whether she should remain in Italy to write her book or return to America. In Italy, she would be able to talk to people involved in the revolution and to learn the background and details of the struggle. She would be sure she had a grasp of all the facts, but her absence from American would make her name less familiar in her own country and might make it more difficult for her to find a publisher. Returning to America would expose her to social awkwardness at times. She knew that many conservative people, some of them her relatives, would disapprove of her marriage to an Italian Catholic. In Italy, her friends were artists and intellectuals more tolerant of differences. The Brownings, who had caused their own scandal by eloping and earning the undying wrath of Elizabeth's father, had no difficulty accepting Margaret's unconventional marriage.

Despite the congenial life in Florence, there were political difficulties. The police kept active surveillance over the couple because of Ossoli's revolutionary activities and he and Margaret were given only three-month permits to remain in the city. There was always a chance their permit might not be renewed, especially after the French army and papal forces became more authoritarian in Rome and insisted revolutionaries should be punished. Finally Margaret decided it was necessary for her to brave the perils of sea travel and the storms of gossip and return to America with her new family.

Even after Margaret decided she and her family should return to America, it took her a long time to make specific plans for leaving. She was enjoying the Italian spring. She wrote:

The Italian spring is as good as Paradise. Days come of glorious sunshine and gently-flowing airs, that expand the heart and uplift the whole nature. The birds are twittering their first notes of love; the ground is enamelled with anemones, cowslips, and crocuses; every old wall and ruin puts on its festoon and garland; and the heavens stoop daily nearer, till the earth is folded in an embrace of light, and her every pulse beats music."

This world is indeed a sad place, despite its sunshine, birds, and crocuses. But I never felt as happy as now, when I always find the glad eyes of my little boy to welcome me. I feel the tie between him and me so real and deep-rooted, that even death shall not part us. So sweet is this unimpassioned love, it knows no dark reactions, it does not idealize, and cannot be daunted by the faults of its object. Nothing but a child can take the worst bitterness out of life, and break the spell of loneliness. I shall not be alone in other worlds, whenever Eternity may call me. (Fuller, Channing, Emerson 1857)

Margaret faced a wrenching decision. The temptation to stay in Italy, where for the first time she was enjoying peaceful family love, was strong, but the difficulties seemed insurmountable. In April the Pope returned to Rome under the protection of the French forces. He was installed in the papal palace amid great celebrations orchestrated by the French. It was clear that Ossoli would not be able to return to Rome for many years because everyone who had participated in the rebellion was deemed a danger to the papacy. And perhaps most pressing of all, Margaret and her family were still poor. With contacts in Rome cut off, Margaret's articles and eventually her book were all they had to support them. Margaret's contacts and hopes of employment were all in America.

The fastest and easiest way to travel to America would have been for the Ossoli family to go to Paris, where Margaret could have visited some friends. Then they could take a packet ship from any one of several French ports. The packet ships, designed to carry mail, traveled swiftly across the Atlantic on a regular schedule and would have reached New York in three or four weeks, but the passage cost about four hundred dollars. Margaret decided they could not afford that. Instead they would travel on a merchant vessel from the Italian city of Leghorn. As Margaret wrote to her brother Richard

The voyage, made in the cheapest way we can, must cost us about 150 dollars as, even if we brave the length and discomforts of voyage by a merchantman, and go without any help for care of the baby in case of being sick, we must still buy stores and have a cow or goat to insure him proper food. We may have in this way two months on the ocean. (Fuller and Hudspeth 1983, 6:66)

Margaret disliked and feared sea travel and there were enough shipwrecks to justify her fears. The first ship she chose for the voyage was lost at sea. She shuddered when she read newspaper accounts of other ships lost on the Atlantic crossing. No matter how carefully she chose a ship, it was a hazardous journey, especially when traveling with a young child. Ossoli, too, did not like the idea of a long sea voyage. As a boy a fortuneteller had told him "Beware of the sea" and he had never in his life set foot in a ship; nonetheless, he accepted the necessity of a trip to America and was willing to follow Margaret anywhere.

Through friends in Florence, Margaret met Captain Seth Hasty, master of the barque Elizabeth, a nearly new American merchantman. Hasty was an experienced New England seaman with a pleasant young wife. On his next trip he would soon be sailing from Leghorn, not far from Florence, with a cargo of old paintings, almonds, olive oil, silk, 150 tons of Carrara marble and a large, bulky statue of John C. Calhoun (Deiss 1969, 304-5). Margaret was impressed by Captain Hasty's knowledge and confidence, so she decided to travel on his ship. The only passengers on the trip would be the Ossolis, Horace Sumner, their Boston friend who had been living in Italy, and a young Italian woman, Celeste Paolini, who was returning to her job as a servant in New York and who agreed to help Margaret take care of Angelino.

Margaret's headaches, which had disappeared during her years in Rome, came back to torment her. Nonetheless she moved ahead preparing for the trip. She packed all of the documents she had acquired in Rome — letters from the American ambassador, the printed edicts of the Republic, letters from Mazzini, and her Roman journal. Her history of Rome was packed separately so she could work on it when she had a chance. She expressed her hopes and fears about her trip home in a long letter to her old friend Emelyn Story:

I find it imperatively necessary to go to the U.S. if I want to have my arrangements made that may free me from care. Will I be more fortunate in person? I do not know, I am ill adapted to push my claims and my pretensions, but at least it will not be such slow work passing from disappointment to disappointment as here where I wait upon the Post Office, and wait two or three months to know the result of any proposition....I go home prepared to expect everything that is painful and difficult. (Fuller and Hudspeth 1983, 6:76)

In that somber spirit, Margaret and her family got ready for the long voyage home.

Chapter 13: Journey Home

On May 17, 1850, the barque *Elizabeth* was ready to sail from the port of Leghorn. As Margaret, Ossoli, and Angelino were rowed in the ship's boat out to the vessel, it must have looked very safe and secure rocking on the gentle waves. The weather was warm the day they sailed and the sea calm and blue. The passenger cabin was located on the deck, so they could get fresh air and some breezes. The cabin had a spacious sitting room and they could also walk around the deck or sit outside in the sunshine. Also traveling on the deck was a goat, partly a pet, which would provide milk for Angelino during the trip. The group was congenial and the Captain and his wife very friendly."

The trip started well as the ship made its way down the Mediterranean toward the Atlantic Ocean. Passengers entertained themselves by having long conversations or playing with the baby; Margaret worked on her manuscript and little Angelino became a favorite of passengers and crew. Celeste was an excellent nursemaid and soon became very fond of the boy. Captain Hasty played with him and told him stories every day and his twenty-six year old wife played her zither and sang to the child. Margaret quietly celebrated her fortieth birthday as the ship sailed through the calm Mediterranean Sea.

On the eighth day out the Captain became ill, suffering from fever and chills. The next day he was worse. He soon developed a rash and a high fever and for the next ten days, he continued to suffer. The travelers soon recognized that he had smallpox, and it turned out to be the most malignant type of the disease. On June 2, the ship anchored off Gibraltar and a steward went ashore to fetch a doctor who might provide some medicine. The man returned without the doctor and with the news that the ship was to be put in quarantine. Officials in the port were afraid of spreading the contagion and no doctor would be allowed aboard nor could any passengers disembark. For two weeks the ship remained anchored just outside the port while Captain Hasty lingered, suffering from a high fever and in agony before he died of smallpox. The crew lowered the ship's flag to half mast to signal his death. Because the authorities refused to let anyone leave the ship, the crew had no choice except to bury him at sea. As other ships in the harbor heard of the death, they all lowered their flags to half mast, and as the sun set, Captain Hasty's body, wrapped in an American flag, was lowered overboard.

After a week, when no one else showed signs of illness, the ship continued on its way. The first mate, Henry Bangs, took charge. Unlike Captain Hasty, Bangs had almost no sailing experience and had to ask Mrs. Hasty for advice, although her experience too was very limited. Two days after they left Gibraltar, little Angelino became ill with the same symptoms that had appeared in Captain Hasty. Margaret was frantic with worry as she and Celeste tended the baby. Fortunately, after a week of illness, the child recovered, perhaps because of the vaccination Margaret had worked so hard to get for him in Italy.

After that the voyage continued quietly day after long summer day as the passengers tried to occupy themselves. Horace Sumner gave Ossoli lessons in English in exchange for Italian lessons and the two struggled to communicate with one another. All through June they sailed and into July. By July 18 the ship was somewhere off the New Jersey coast. Mr. Bangs announced they would land in New York the next day and the passengers packed their trunks for landing.

During the night a storm came up, but Bangs, believing they were off the coast of New Jersey, held his course. Unfortunately he was wrong about their location. He had mistaken the Fire Island lighthouse for one in New Jersey and headed northeast toward what he thought was New York Harbor. At about four o'clock in the morning the ship struck a sandbar off the shore of Fire Island. Only then did he realize that instead of heading toward New Jersey, they were off the coast of Long Island, New York, about thirty miles north of where he thought they were. Here the currents were always dangerous and the surf deadly.

At the first jar, the passengers, who had been trying to sleep, sprang from their berths. Soon they heard a crew member shout, "Cut away" followed by the crash of falling timbers as the main and mizzen mast were cut free. Then they heard the thunder of the seas, as they broke across the deck. In a moment more, the cabin skylight was dashed in pieces by the breakers, and the spray, pouring down like a cataract, put out the lights, while the cabin door was wrenched from its fastenings, and the waves swept in and out. The ship struck the shore twice more and on the second shock, the marble statue of Calhoun, stored in the hold, smashed through the bottom. Passengers were thrown out of their bunks. Water rushed in through the hole and swirled across the decks.

The passengers gathered together in the cabin and hoped dawn would come before the ship went down. They did not know where they were or how far from shore. For three hours they huddled together in the darkness.

Finally daylight came, but the scene was desolate. They were only a few hundred yards from shore, but separated from it by high, turbulent waves. The ship's lifeboats had been swept out to sea and only one life preserver remained. That went to a seaman who volunteered to swim ashore for help. An hour went by and no lifeboat appeared, so they had to assume the man had not made it to shore. On the shore they could see a wagon and some men picking up wreckage from the storm. The passengers and crew on the Elizabeth waved frantically to signal their need for help, but the men on the beach paid no attention. They were beach pirates hunting for wreckage, a major source of income for many Long Islanders. They made no attempt to rescue the people on the ship and scarcely looked up to see whether anyone was trying to swim ashore.

At that time there was no system of paid rescuers on the Long Island shore. The only rescue device in the vicinity was a lifeboat with a mortar to fire a lifeline across a stretch of water. These were stored at the Fire Island lighthouse three miles away, about an hour's walk. The lifeboat required eight to ten men to carry it along the sandy shore. The lighthouse keeper finally got men to move the equipment but it didn't reach the beach until between twelve and one o'clock, more than eight hours after the Elizabeth was stranded, and more than six hours after the wreck could easily have been seen. When the lifeboat finally arrived, the beach men could not be persuaded to launch or man her. No doubt it was a daunting task. Waves were high and the chances of their safely launching the boat directly into a headwind were slight. The potential rescuers, most of whom had probably seen friends and family members drown in rough surf, insisted it was too dangerous to attempt the launch.

Aboard the ship, a few passengers decided to use one of the planks strewn around the deck as a life raft. Mrs. Hasty was the first to go, clinging to a plank and attempting to swim to shore. Eventually she reached the beach, exhausted and almost unconscious. Horace Sumner tried next, but he sank and drowned.

Margaret refused to leave her family and try the swim to shore; Ossoli declared he would stay with her. After trying vainly to persuade them to leave, Captain Bangs ordered the crew to save themselves rather than face certain death in a sinking ship. Three crew members remained on board and tried to persuade Celeste, Ossoli, and Margaret to take a plank and attempt the trip. Finally the ship swung broadside to the waves and the battering grew worse. The steward begged Margaret to let him try to make it to shore with the baby, and finally she agreed. She handed over the baby and stood, wrapped in her large white shawl looking shoreward as the steward took Angelino in his arms, seized a plank, and jumped into the water. Just then a large wave struck the ship and as the deck tilted upwards, Celeste, Ossoli, and Margaret disappeared from sight. After a few minutes in the water, the seaman was separated from

Angelino and twenty minutes later both of their bodies were washed up on the beach.

The bodies of Margaret and Ossoli were never found. Some of their belongings washed up on shore — a few bits of clothing and a small trunk containing a packet of love letters and other family papers. For several hours waves continued to batter the shore until gradually the storm subsided. When the sea finally calmed, the hull of the Elizabeth, with the foremast still bound to it by cordage, lay so near the shore that it looked as if a dozen oar-strokes would have carried a boat alongside. The ship glittered in the sunshine and rocked gently in the swell. One of the first visitors to see the scene of the wreck wrote in his diary that seven resolute men might have saved every soul on board, but those brave rescuers never appeared. Margaret Fuller's life and the lives of her husband and son were cut short within sight of the shore they longed to reach.

Chapter 14: Reverberations

Margaret's family, who had been waiting for her return, received instead the news of her death. They rushed to New York where Margaret's mother and sister stayed with the Springs in Brooklyn while her brothers and brother-in-law joined the search for remains on the Fire Island shore. Rebecca Spring recalled later that Margaret's mother "shed no tears, she even smiled when we spoke to her, but she neither ate nor slept,--it was pitiful." (Capper 2007, 512)

Emerson considered going to Long Island to join the search, but decided to send the younger and more energetic Henry Thoreau instead. When Thoreau arrived on July 25, wreckage from the ship — planks, clothing and opened trunks littered the sand. Thoreau walked up and down the beach searching for some trace of Margaret or her family. Aside from fragments of lumber and water-soaked letters, all he found was one button apparently ripped from Ossoli's jacket. He gave it to Margaret's mother as a grim memento.

The tiny body of Angelino Ossoli was discovered by some seamen from the ship who buried it carefully in the dunes. Months later the body was sent to Margaret's mother who arranged burial in Mount Auburn cemetery in Cambridge, Massachusetts. In 1853, the family bought a larger plot that could hold a memorial to Timothy Fuller as well as one for the Ossoli family. The memorial portrays a book to indicate Margaret's literary interests and the hilt of a sword marking Ossoli as a soldier. Angelino's tiny body was buried at the base of the stone.

As Mount Auburn cemetery, the first garden cemetery in the country, grew as a tourist attraction, a picture of the memorial was featured in the guide book to Mount Auburn. Visitors often stopped by to see the graves and for many years the location was mentioned as a favorite contemplation spot in the well-known cemetery.

During the days after the wreck, Thoreau joined Charles Sumner, brother of Horace, in interviewing survivors from the wreck. Gradually the story of the wreck came out. Of the 23 persons on board, eight were lost including all of the passengers. Although crewmembers had struggled to save all the passengers, Margaret and her family remained adamant about not leaving the ship. Captain Bangs had no choice except to order his men to save their own lives because there was nothing more they could do to save their passengers. Even then one sailor endangered himself by insisting on taking Angelino and trying to get him to shore.

When Thoreau and Sumner arrived, they found that during the weekend almost a thousand people had visited the two-mile stretch of beach, which had been strewn with wreckage. A few might have found souvenirs or some small items to sell or use. Certainly almost nothing of value was left—only empty bags of almonds and scraps of clothing and paper remained on the sand.

The two men interviewed survivors of the wreck and Mrs. Hasty gave them many details about what happened on the ship during that last wild storm. Thoreau located several people who lived in the area of the wreck and was not impressed by their efforts to help the survivors. Smith Oates, who lived on the island in what Thoreau described as "a perfect pirate's house" of stolen good and debris, had frequently been arrested for stealing cargo from wrecks. He claimed to have slept through most of the excitement of the wreck, but Thoreau was suspicious. In his notebooks Thoreau wrote: "There were thieves of high and low degree whose deeds were described to me by themselves...They stole from one another extensively — and whatever a guard placed over it, they rolled across the beach to their boats in the night." (Capper 2007, 502) So for hours on the morning of the wreck — from seven o'clock to eleven — they paid no attention to the ship or its passengers and crew but gathered up all the clothing and merchandise they could find.

Thoreau and Sumner searched diligently but it was almost impossible to know how much was missing or to identify belongings. During a trip to the nearby town of Patchogue a few days after the wreck, Thoreau visited a home where two young men were playing dominoes and wearing hats decorated with tassels and buttons which Thoreau strongly suspected were from Margaret's dresses.

Margaret Fuller's death made headlines in New York and Boston. Horace Greeley's *New York Tribune* announced "FATAL WRECK — Dreadful loss of life — S. Margaret Fuller Drowned" (Capper 2007, 512). Other newspapers quickly picked up the story, but none covered it as fully as Greeley did. Greeley wrote a series of editorials calling on the government to punish the pirates who had stolen property from the wreck and to set up a "life-saving system on the coast" to prevent future events of this kind

The sudden burst of newspaper publicity about Margaret's death surprised the beach pirates and the seamen who had refused to take the lifeboat out into the storm. One of them told Sumner, "Oh if we had known there were any such persons of importance on board, we should have tried our best." In all fairness, launching a lifeboat in the turbulent waves would have been extremely dangerous and the Islanders who saw several wrecks every year were painfully familiar with the horrors of drowning. Immigrant ships from Europe heading for New York were especially vulnerable. Only four years earlier, the barque *Bristol* with 100 Irish immigrants from Liverpool was wrecked in heavy fog and 84 of the passengers drowned.

Although wrecks were frequent along the coast of Long Island, the attention of Margaret's eminent and articulate friends called public attention to this type of disaster. Horace Greeley's voice calling for reform of lighthouse and lifesaving services was added to that of many others. Eventually this led to the establishment of the United States Lighthouse Service in 1852. Greeley also had the satisfaction of knowing some of the scavengers, including Oates, were arrested for stealing property from the Elizabeth.

While her friends were still searching for traces of Margaret's life and possessions, news of her death was spreading. Interest was greatest in New England, of course, but throughout the country, newspapers and magazines took notice and most of the reports praised her writing and her ideas. In the *Southern Literary Messenger*, a commentator wrote, "I am happy to notice that since her stormy exit with scarce a single exception, the presses that were the loudest in her vituperation , are prompt to do her the most delicate and cordial justice to her memory." Even in Rome, the announcement of her death filled Romans "with a degree of sorrow, which is not often bestowed upon a foreigner, and, especially, one of a different faith." (Capper 2007, 515)

Among acquaintances in Boston, some reactions were more mixed. Many conservatives had never approved of Margaret's radical ideas and outspoken criticism of conventional life. Her support of revolution in Italy was viewed with suspicion and her surprising marriage to a foreigner was seen as a fall from virtuous American life. Octavius Frothingham, a liberal Unitarian clergyman, reported that "When the news of her death reached Boston, one of Boston's eminent men in letters and public affairs quietly remarked: 'it is just as well so'" (Capper 2007, 515) Margaret had offended some women by her support for women's rights and they had never been able to accept the social freedom she encouraged. The fastidious and timid Sophia Hawthorne wrote, "I am really glad she died. There was no other peace or rest to be found for her — especially if her husband was a person so wanting in force and availability." Sophia's sister Mary agreed that Ossoli "was wholly unfit to be her husband in this country, although he might have answered in Italy." (Capper 2007, 517) More than a century later, it is difficult to understand why Margaret was seen as a threat to the established pattern of American life. She had taken the radical ideas of the New England transcendentalists and applied them to a carefully regulated society. Should men learn to trust themselves and not look back to history? Then why shouldn't Italian patriots throw off the yoke of clerical rule? Should each man live a life of self-reliance? Then why shouldn't Irish immigrants dream of establishing successful dynasties in America? More than that, she had extended this freedom to women. She dreamed of women becoming leaders. It was easy to see her as a threat to the quiet currents of life in New England.

Some of the people who had known her best acknowledged the loss of an important critic of society and literature. In his journal Emerson summed up the tragedy of her life: "To the last her country proves inhospitable to her; brave; eloquent, subtle, accomplished, devoted, constant soul! If nature availed in America to give birth to many such as she, freedom and honour and letters and art too were safe in this new world." In a more personal vein he noted "I have lost in her my audience". (Von Mehren 1994, 338) James Freeman Clarke too mourned her loss and the fact that America seemed to have no place for a woman like her: "There seems no position for her like, and her life was complete as far as experiences and development went." (Von Mehren 1994, 338)

As the years went by, Margaret Fuller's reputation has fluctuated with changing times. Soon after her death, a group of friends led by Emerson proposed a biography should be written. The family was happy to cooperate. In the end it was William Channing, James Freeman Clarke, and Emerson who gathered Margaret's papers and prepared Fuller, Channing, and Emerson 1857. The three friends, all of them ordained ministers, were eager to avoid controversy and they felt no need to preserve the records as Margaret wrote them. They cut large sections out of the journals and letters so no breath of scandal would injure Margaret's reputation and her more radical political ideas would be hidden. The question of whether to talk about her marriage at all caused them so much anxiety that they mentioned it only briefly.

Somewhat to Emerson's surprise, the book sold well. The first 1000 copies were gone in 24 hours. It continued to sell well for several years until the beginnings of the Civil War turned attention toward the harsh reality of an endangered country. After the war there were more editions, thirteen including a translation into German, before the end of the century.

Twenty years after Margaret's death, a group of her friends gathered to hold a commemorative sixtieth birthday party for her. Old friends shared memories of her life and its impact on them and Julia Ward Howe read a poem she had written for the occasion.

Margaret Fuller, although she lived only forty years, had a lasting impact on American society. Her career as a journalist and writer showed that women could be active and influence people and events. Through the series of conversations she arranged, she inspired women to read and think for themselves rather than looking to men for guidance. The first generation of American feminists who fought for the right of women to own property, to vote, and to compete with men in professional and business life was strongly influenced by Margaret's work.

Elizabeth Cady Stanton, one of the most important early feminists, had attended a series of Margaret's conversations when she was a young bride. In 1848, after the first women's rights convention in Seneca Falls, she wrote in the Declaration of Sentiments:

Resolved, That all laws which prevent women from occupying such a station in society as her conscience shall dictate, or which place her in a position inferior to that of man, are contrary to the great precept of nature, and therefore of no force or authority.

That declaration echoed and built on Margaret's ideas from *Women in the Nineteenth Century*. Many women continued to struggle for women's rights and all of them owed something to the ideas first expressed by Margaret Fuller. Almost a hundred years later after Fuller's death, in 1930, Eleanor Roosevelt acknowledged the importance of Margaret's influence on successive generations of women:

"Her book, *Women in the Nineteenth Century*, was an epoch-making book and her power to impress her personality and her greatness of soul on those around her did more than anything else to bring the acknowledgment and the recognition that women had an intellectual and spiritual contribution to make, as great as that of men." (Bell 1930, 14)

New England was too small a stage for Margaret Fuller to play out her life. Her vision took her beyond the narrow confines of Massachusetts to the wider view inscribed on her cenotaph in Mount Auburn cemetery. *Born a child of New England - By adoption a citizen of Rome - By genius belonging to the World.*

"Let them be sea captains," Margaret wrote, and many people laughed, but her ideas prevailed. Now, when women are airplane pilots and astronauts, they are carrying out Margaret's vision. Soon after Margaret finished *Women in the Nineteenth Century*, she wrote, "I had put a good deal of my true life in it, as if, suppose I went away now, the measure of my foot-print would be left on the earth." (Fuller and Hudspeth 1983, 3:241) Her footprint has indeed been left and has changed the lives of generations of women who came after her.

Sources Cited

Alcott, Amos Bronson. 1837. *Conversations with Children on the Gospels*. Boston: J. Munroe and Company.

Baker, Carlos. 1996. *Emerson among the Eccentrics: A Group Portrait*. Intro. and epilogue by James R. Mellow. NY: Penguin Books.

Bell, Margaret. 1930. *Margaret Fuller: A Biography*. New York: Charles Boni.

Bolster, Arthur S. Jr. 1954. *James Freeman Clarke; Disciple to Advancing Truth*. Boston: Beacon Press.

Capper, Charles. 1992. *Margaret Fuller: An American Romantic Life: The Private Years*. New York: Oxford University Press.

Capper, Charles. 2007. *Margaret Fuller: An American Romantic Life: The Public Years*. New York: Oxford University Press.

Chevigny, Bell Gale, and Fuller, Margaret. 1976. *The Woman and the Myth: Margaret Fuller's Life and Writings*. Old Westbury, N.Y.: Feminist Press.

Cooke, George Willis. 1961. *The Dial: An Historical and Biographical Introduction to Accompany*. Reprint ed. 2 vols. NY: Russell & Russell. Original edition, 1902.

Dall, Caroline Wells Healey, and Margaret Fuller. 1895. *Margaret and her Friends;* Boston: Roberts Brothers.

Deiss, Joseph Jay. 1969. *The Roman Years of Margaret Fuller; a Biography*. New York: Crowell.

Emerson, Ralph Waldo. 1940. *The Complete Essays and Other Writings of Ralph Waldo Emerson.* New York: Modern Library.

Emerson, Ralph Waldo. 1960. *Journals and Miscellaneous Notebooks of Ralph Waldo Emerson* edited by Gilman, William H. 16 vols. Cambridge MA: Belknap Press of Harvard University.

Fuller, Margaret. 1991. *Summer on the Lakes in 1843,* Prairie State books. Urbana: University of Illinois Press.

Fuller, Margaret, Larry Joe Reynolds, and Susan Belasco Smith. 1991. *These Sad but Glorious Days: Dispatches from Europe, 1846-1850.* New Haven: Yale University Press.

Fuller, Margaret, and Arthur B. Fuller. 1860. *At Home and Abroad, or, Things and Thoughts in America and Europe.* Boston: Brown Taggard and Chase.

Fuller, Margaret, Judith Mattson Bean, and Joel Myerson. 2000. *Margaret Fuller, Critic: Writings from the New-York Tribune, 1844-1846.* New York: Columbia University Press.

Fuller, Margaret, William Henry Channing, and Ralph Waldo Emerson. *Memoirs of Margaret Fuller Ossoli.* Original publication: Boston: Phillips, Sampson and Company, 1857.

Fuller, Margaret, and Robert N. Hudspeth. 1983. *The Letters of Margaret Fuller.* 6 volumes. Ithaca, N.Y.: Cornell University Press.

Fuller, Margaret, and Mary Kelley. 1994. *The Portable Margaret Fuller,* Viking Portable Library. New York: Penguin Books.

Fuller, Margaret, Arthur B. Fuller, and Bernard Rosenthal. 1971. *Woman in the Nineteenth Century,* Norton Library, N615. New York: Norton.

Greenough, Horatio. 1887. *Letters of Horatio Greenough to His Brother, Henry Greenough.* Ed. by Frances Boott Greenough. Boston: Ticknor.

Higginson, Thomas Wentworth. *Margaret Fuller Ossoli.* 1899. American Men of Letters. Edited by C. D. Warner. Boston: Houghton Mifflin.

Fuller, Margaret, and James Gotendorf. 1903. *Love-letters of Margaret Fuller, 1845-1846.* New York: D. Appleton and Company.

Marraro, Howard R. 1932. *American Opinion on the Unification of Italy 1846-1861.* New York: Columbia Univ. Press.

Mickiewicz, Adam. 1917. *Sonnets from the Crimea.* Translated by Edna Worthley Underwood. San Francisco: Paul Elder & Co.

Miller, Edwin Haviland. 1991. *Salem Is My Dwelling Place: A Life of Nathaniel Hawthorne.* Iowa City: University of Iowa Press.

Poe, Edgar Allen. 1846. "Literati of New York City-No. IV" In *Godey's Lady's Book*, 72-78.

Rapport, Mike. 2008. *1848: Year of Revolution.* New York: Basic Books.

Seitz, Don Carlos. 1926. *Horace Greeley, Founder of The New York Tribune.* Indianapolis: Bobbs-Merrill.

Trollope, Frances. 1836. *Paris and the Parisians in 1835.* New York: Harper.

Von Mehren, Joan. 1994. *Minerva and the Muse: a Life of Margaret Fuller.* Amherst: University of Massachusetts Press.

###

Connect with me online
My blog: www.teacupsandtyrants.com

Printed in Great Britain
by Amazon